ANTIQUES
An Illustrated A–Z

THERLE HUGHES

ANTIQUES

AN ILLUSTRATED

A to Z

MacGibbon & Kee London

Granada Publishing Limited
First published in Great Britain 1971 by MacGibbon & Kee Ltd
3 Upper James Street London WIR 4BP

Copyright © 1971 by Therle Hughes

ISBN O 261 63231 O
Printed in Great Britain by Cox & Wyman Ltd
London, Fakenham and Reading

INTRODUCTION

'The world is so full of a number of things,
I'm sure we should all be as happy as kings.'

If only the self-styled experts did not entangle even the simplest and loveliest things in technical terms, historical allusions, sometimes almost a secret language. All too easily that may mean exclusion for the rest of us. Yet today our pleasure can be wider-ranging than ever before and correspondingly rewarding.

This book is intended merely to furnish a little of the basic background language that can open the way for the many who wish to include yesterday's 'things' among their pleasures. This implies at least a glimpse into yesterday's ideas of design and craftsmanship, at least a first step to the understanding of materials and the techniques men have developed to coax them into use and beauty. Today, with so many great houses, museums, studios, factories throwing open their doors to us, it is pity indeed if our own comprehension gap keeps us from revelling in their welcome.

Here are basic terms, names, details of techniques concerning earlier centuries' furniture, metal wares, ceramics and many other homely items that I have found essential to my own researches, illustrated wherever I have thought this might aid understanding or identification and fully numbered for cross reference. Words are fined down to a minimum so that I have been able to include well over 1000 entries (half of them illustrated). But this implies in the reader a realisation, for example, that much silverware was widely imitated in cheaper metals, culminating in later Victorian electro-plate, and that yesterday's pieces of porcelain are few indeed compared with England's brilliantly successful bone china.

My dates indicate the approximate introduction of items *in Great Britain* but it is seldom possible to indicate when – if ever – production ceased. Here I have taken the story through Victorian days to the beginning of the 20th century – that is to 1901. Moreover I should be the first to admit the skill of our Victorian great-grandparents in confusing every subject with their sophisticated replicas as well as happy-to-lucky 'improvements' on past design. On this, briefly, I can only say: if an article has features suggesting different periods it is seldom earlier than the 19th century.

Preparation of this book has taken me along many delightful byways. I shall feel it has been worth while as well as enjoyable if even a few of my many enthusiastic correspondents find here the spark that fires them to seek further enlightenment and pleasure, whether among dessert glasses or barometers, posy holders or piecrust wares, vinaigrettes or pearl-encrusted papier mâché.

ANTIQUES
An Illustrated A-Z

Abbotsford furniture Mainly 1830s–60s. Collectors' name for furnishings in romantic-Gothic mood inspired by novels of Sir Walter Scott (1771–1832) often with ill-proportioned distortions of Elizabethan and Carolean features such as massively carved cabinets, bulbous legs and twist turning (**1**). Scott's 'library was the precursor of innumerable picturesquely furnished English houses.' (G. A. Scala, 1868.)

Acanthus From classic Greek architecture. On furniture, metal work, stylised thistle-like foliage, much indented, carved on brackets, cabriole knees. (Sheraton example **123**.)

Act of Parliament clock See *Coaching inn clock*.

Adam brothers Influential 1760–1800s. John, Robert, James and William: Robert (1728–92), architect and designer, the most important, was the immensely successful promoter of neo-classic style in the English home.

Adams family From 1657 to present day. Important Staffordshire potters. Included: William (1746–1805), notable jasper ware; Benjamin (at work 1805–12), exceptionally fine blue-printed ware; William (1772–1829), bone china and earthenware, his printed wares for export now highly valuable; William (1798–1873), including jasper, parian busts of celebrities.

Adze marks Medieval and later. Irregular ridges and saucer-shaped hollows on surfaces of furniture which have been levelled by type of axe with cutting edge at right angles to haft.

Agate ware Especially from 1740s onwards, associated with Thomas Whieldon, and in late 19th century. Stoneware and earthenware imitating veined agate. Made by intermingling clays that burnt to different colours so that the

1 Abbotsford chair

2 Agate ware teapot, *c.* 1740s

9

3   Ale glass with hop and barley engraving

4   Ale warmer, boot shape

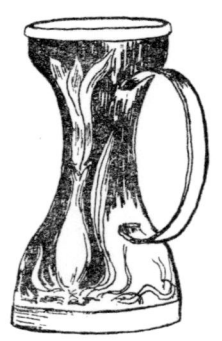

5   Aller Vale crocus vase

6   Amelia of cut and pricked paper

veining extended throughout the body of the ware (2, 220 right).

Air twist   Especially 1735–60. Glass. Bubbles of air elongated into thread-like spirals within the stem of drinking glass. Quality improved c. 1750. See also *Mercury twist*.

Ale glass   From 1680s onwards in flint-glass. Drinking glass with deep conical bowl (3). From c. 1740s hop-and-barley ornament often distinguished the vessel for sparkling, potent strong-ale from cider glass (179).

Ale warmer   Usually 18th–19th century. Copper or brass, tinned inside, for hot drinks. Cone-shaped with long handle for pushing into a grate fire; boot shaped for primitive down-hearth fire (4). Now reproduced.

Aller Vale ware   1868–1901. Devonshire. At first, cheap fireclay garden ornaments. From 1887, as Aller Vale Art Potteries, vessels in red clay with incised ornament cut into ground of yellow slip and popular crocus vases in blue, green, cream and gold (5).

Amber   Timeless; popular with late Victorians. Fossilised resin of prehistoric trees in warm yellowish tones, very light and warm to touch. Used for jewellery, ornaments, posy holders, desk furnishings and so on.

Amberina glass   Late 19th century. Translucent flint-glass, with air bubbles, showing colour variation, heat-induced, through shades of red and warm yellows. Trinket vessels, ornament.

Amelias   From 1830. Hobby for young ladies popularised by invalid Amelia Blackburn. Pictures such as exotic birds, flower garlands, constructed of minute paper fragments cut, gummed and painted to achieve naturalistic effects of texture and shading (6). Basis of thick paper, the motifs being given substance by needle pricking from the back. See also *Pricked pictures*.

American views in Staffordshire blue   Especially c. 1816–40. Staffordshire earthenware, transfer-printed with over 750 views, portraits, historical incidents. Vastly exported by about twenty potteries and now valuable (517).

Amorini   Usually 'boys' in contemporaneous records. Like putti, Italian term now applied to winged cupids as, e.g. furniture ornament. Cherubs might be winged heads.

Andirons (firedogs) From Roman days to 18th century. Iron; more rarely silver, bronze, latten, brass and later steel. Pair of L-shaped bars with decorative uprights (standards) flanking log-burning hearth (**7**). Usually wrought iron until early 16th century, then usually cast and more massive. In 18th century incorporated in dog-grate (**93**).

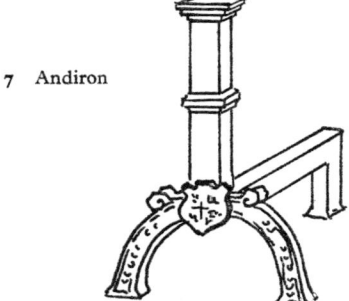

7 Andiron

8 Angel bed, 18th century

Aneroid barometer From 1844. Compact, portable, circular, cheap. Atmospheric pressure measured by its effect on shallow chamber, hermetically sealed, exhausted of air and partly elastic. Eventually displaced mercury-tube barometers.

Angel bed From end of 17th century. With curtain-hung tester supported only at the head, without footposts (**8**). Popular in 19th century, extending over only half the bed.

Annealing Glass process. Essential slow heating to toughen flint-glass. Improved methods 1740s and 1780s promoted introduction of increasingly ambitious cut ornament. See also *Lehr*.

9 Three versions of anthemion motif

Anthemion Ornament of formalised honeysuckle flower from Grecian architecture (**9**: three styles from Regency).

Appliqué work One of the oldest forms of textile ornament. Bold patterns formed by stitching fabric motifs to contrasting fabric grounds. Church and home furnishings, banners, horse trappings.

Apron Furniture. Ornamentally shaped wood between front legs immediately below the cross-framing of table (**10**), chair-seat or chest-furniture. Also on silver such as tea-kettle stand.

10 Apron, carved wood, on side table

Aquatint From late 1760s. Print suggesting wash drawing on rough paper rather than depending on hard outlines: method of giving surface tone to etching. The printing plate was prepared for its acid etching by being given a texture, most often a covering of porous resin, so that the acid recorded its 'grain'. Easy basis for commercial colourist. Paul Sandby (1725–1809) was notable English exponent (*c.* 1775–83) though not originator.

Arabesque Classical ornament, revived by Renaissance, popular with Victorians. Foliage, flowers, in elaborate intertwinings **(205)**. On furniture such as marquetry and low relief carving on English chest and cabinet work.

Arcaded ornament Especially late 16th century to 1670s on English furniture. Series of arches carved in relief on vertical face of chest or bedstead, suggesting architectural arcade.

Architect's table From 1750s into 19th century. Drawing or writing table **(11)**. The top can be raised to a slant. Below, the front extends forward as a deep drawer, part of the front legs moving with it for steadiness and with a sliding lid to write on and a quadrant till for inks.

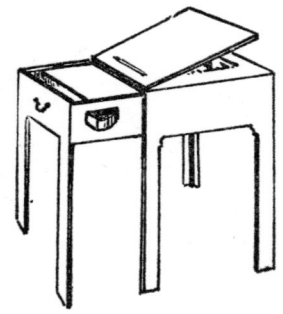

11   Architect's table with top raised and drawer pulled forward

Argentan plate See *German silver*.

Argyle From 1760s to early 19th century. Silver, Sheffield plate. Suggesting ill-proportioned, thin-spouted teapot. Divided internally so that gravy is kept hot inside a hot water lining **(12)** or around a central box-iron.

12   Argyle, with hot water lining filled at top of handle

Armada chest Late 17th–18th centuries. Furniture. English name for heavy iron strong box with elaborate lock.

Art nouveau End of 19th century, from Continent. Brief fashion in interior decoration with emphasis on vertical lines; much use of light rosewood with metal, glass, shell and other materials in low relief. Excessively tall spindly furniture and art wares **(13)** with heart-shaped apertures and squirming, up-thrusting plant ornament.

Arts and crafts movement Through 1880s–90s. Supported by such important designers as Walter Crane, Lewis Day, William De Morgan. Now especially associated with 20th-century-approved country-plain furniture and pastel-toned art pottery, but fascinating in complexity with many possibilities for tomorrow's collectors. Conflicting aims of numerous influential guilds and groups expressed in series of exhibitions from 1888: revival of Gothic medievalism variously interpreted and of 'Queen Anne' 18th-century elegance, involving wide range of crafts and materials in home decoration. Commercially, led to over-emphasis of a few easily expressed features such as *art nouveau's* shoddy 'quaint' style.

Art Union of London Established 1836. Subscribing members joined in annual draw for works of art, including many minor prizes such as specially-commissioned (and marked) parian statuary, Doulton stoneware and engravings. So successful that several provincial cities launched similar schemes.

13 Art nouveau jug, typical shape and ornament

Astbury ware Around 1730s–40s. Crude, lively hand-modelled figures in brown and white clays, such as *pew groups* (q.v.) **(14)** unmarked but now attributed to John and Thomas Astbury who made various earthenwares through 18th century.

Automata Figures driven by clockwork. Timeless in simple forms; with musical accompaniment from 18th century; with elaborate music from 1810. Dancing dolls, silent from *c.* 1810; on musical boxes from 1860. Monkey antics from *c.* 1850. Celebrated English makers include Christopher Pinchbeck (early 18th century) and James Cox, at work from 1760.

Aventurine Form of quartz, glittering with mica, widely imitated in brownish glass flecked with gold-coloured spangles, for 18th-century comfit box lids and the like. Imitations, as early as 17th century with fragments of gold wire in japanning varnish. Popular Victorian imitation composed of flint-glass fused with iron filings.

Axminster carpet From 1755. Seamless hand-knotted pile carpet in Turkish style, originated by weaver Thomas Whitty. In 1835 looms moved from Axminster, Devon, to Wilton.

14 Astbury ware pew group

Backstool   Some Elizabethan; mainly 17th–18th centuries. Resembling a single (i.e. armless) chair but of different construction, with four identical legs and stool-like seat, for sitting back-to-room at card-table or dressing-table (**15**).

Bail Handle   Especially 18th century. Half-hoop swinging handle, its ends turning within knobs. Decorative detail in silver cake baskets, epergnes. In brass, in changing, datable styles on 18th-century furniture (**16**: Queen Anne to George III).

Baillie, Lady Grizell   Remembered for her household accounts, 1692–1733: fascinating record of family spending, covering travel, children's education, servant costs (eight different cooks in 1715), fashion, and shopping that ranged from japanned furniture to snuff handkerchiefs and her grandchild's thread mittens.

Ball-and-claw foot   Fashionable in second quarter of 18th century. Furniture (**141**), silver. Collectors distinguish between contemporaneous ball-and-claw and lion paw (**17**), and the more formalised Regency paw (**359**). Long retained in everyday furniture and popular, poorly shaped, on reproductions.

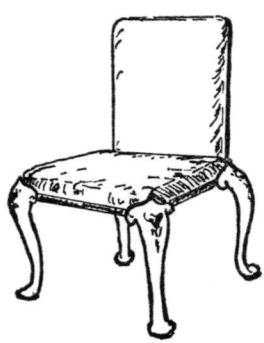

15   Backstool with matching cabriole legs

16   Bail handles: successive shapes, Queen Anne to George III

17   Two ball-and-claw feet, one webbed, and lion paw

Balloon back chair 1820s–50s. Upper back shaped as open oval, often dipped at top centre, supported by short, nipped-in side rails (**18**). Usually heavy Greek front legs.

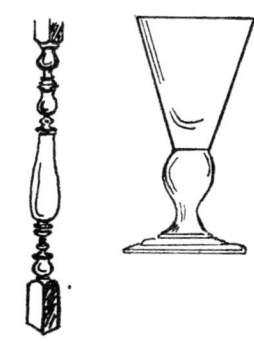

19   Baluster leg and baluster stem glass

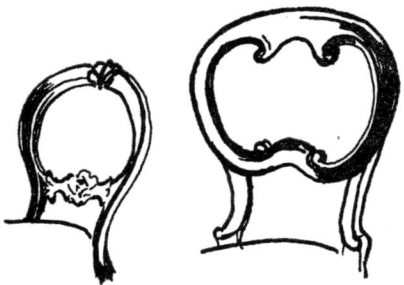

18   Two typical balloon chair backs

Baluster Especially 17th–early 18th centuries and country work into 19th century. Furniture. Turned wood railing in vase outline. Legs of chairs, gate-leg tables (**19**; pilaster **324** *right*). Hence baluster-back chair with flat splat in similar outline. Tiny baluster spindles for tray, table and cabinet galleries, later 18th and 19th centuries.

Baluster glass About 1685–1760. Drinking glass with swelling stem in vase shape (**19, 239, 434**); sometimes inverted or double baluster. Lighter style from *c.* 1725.

Bamboo furniture Some late 18th century; more Regency and post-Regency and again in late 19th century (**20**: canterbury), especially for minor rooms. Giant Indian reed imitated in beech and other cheap woods often turned and stained (occasionally cast iron).

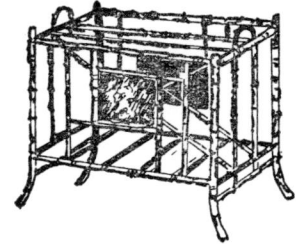

20   Bamboo canterbury, Victorian

Bamboo ware About 1770 onwards. Fine-stoneware evolved by Josiah Wedgwood and shaped into vessels suggesting lengths of bamboo lashed together with cane (**21, 68**). Sometimes touched with colour, including red from *c.* 1800.

21   Bamboo ware teapot, *c.* 1790s

Banded ware From 18th century. Simple horizontal lines of colour painted on cheap earthenware vessels such as mugs, vases, perceptible to the touch. Freehand work until early 19th century.

Banjo barometer Popular 1775–late 19th century. Wheel or dial type set in banjo- or pear-shaped case (mahogany or rosewood) with minor dials above (**22**); often a clock and spirit level from *c.* 1800. Late specimens fitted with *aneroid barometers* (q.v.).

22   Banjo barometer with thermometer and hygrometer

23 Banner firescreen

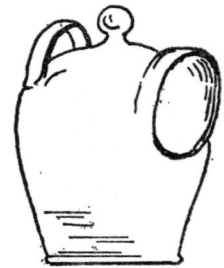

24 Barm pot

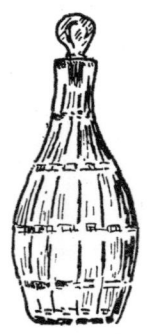

25 Barrel decanter, *c.* 1780s

26 Basaltes, Wedgwood dolphin bowl

Banner firescreen 1790s onwards. Pole-screen with heavy fabric or beadwork, often fringed, hanging loosely from an adjustable cross-bar **(23)**.

Banquet From late 17th century. Elegant informal repast of fruits and sweetmeats popular with Georgians as a dessert. See also *Dessert glasses.*

Barm pot Traditional. Earthenware vessel for yeast. Also for salt (salt kit). One-piece vessel, its contents protected by domed top, but accessible by hand-size opening high in side **(24)**.

Baroque style Late 17th–early 18th centuries. Term now applied to massive, florid furnishings lavishly carved, from Charles II chairs to George I console tables. Lacked light touch of succeeding rococo style.

Barrel design 1770s–1800s. Swelling, flat-bottomed shape of staved and hooped barrel. Introduced by silversmiths (e.g. beakers) and copied especially in glass decanters **(25)** (advertised 1775), fluted porcelain tea jars, earthenware mugs and so on.

Basaltes From mid-1760s. Fine-stoneware, unglazed. Wedgwood's improvement on earlier Egyptian black stoneware. Glowing black vases **(26)**, figures, tea-ware. Also made by Turner, Neale & Palmer and others. Term black-basalt usually given to modern work.

Bas-relief Especially 1760s–1830s. Ornament in less than half relief. Associated with neoclassic style in furniture medallions and paterae and in stoneware ornament shaped separately in small moulds and 'sprigged' on to the unfired surface.

Bateman silver About 1770–1815. Typical medium quality domestic silver **(27)** from factory developed by Hester Bateman (widowed 1760, d. 1794) rather than her

27 Bateman silver gravy boat with detail of maker's mark

personal work. Aided by sons John, Peter, William, Jonathan, and Jonathan's wife Ann. Mark to 1790 (when Hester retired) cursive H.B. (**27 right**), then $\frac{PB}{IB}$ (Jonathan d. 1791); then $\frac{PB}{AB}$ for Peter and Ann. From 1815 William Bateman was proprietor.

Bat's-wing fluting Especially late 18th–early 19th centuries (**28**). Silver ornament: a series of shallow channels curved and graduated to fit, for example, a vessel's rounded foot. Each channel ends in a dipping or concave arc – the opposite to petal fluting.

28 Bat's-wing fluting on silver teapot

Battam, T. At work 1840s–60s. Notable decorator of huge terracotta vases and urns in Etruscan manner (**157**), such as classical figure scenes, at first in black on buff or red ground; later also in red on black ground. See also *Terracotta*.

Battersea enamels 1753–6. Opaque white enamel fused on to thin core of copper and metal-mounted to form snuff box, etui and so on, decorated mainly by delicate monochrome transfer-printing (**514**). Many *Bilston, Wednesbury* and *Birmingham enamels* (q.v.) now wrongly credited to Battersea. Little is known of earlier painted enamels made in London in the 1740s.

Baxter prints 1836–57. Colour prints suggesting oil paintings, made from a succession of blocks superimposed, the process patented in 1836 by George Baxter (1804–67). Mounted labelled prints can be dated closely. Wide range of quality. In 1868, 69 sets of blocks acquired and used by *A. Le Blond* (q.v.), known as Le Blond-Baxters.

Bead work From 13th century; English-made beads from 17th century. Book-covers, glove ornament and so on. 1640s–80s frequently pictorial, couched to fabric and sometimes padded (**29**: details from 17th-century cushion). From 1760s, extremely bright small beads for purses, bags. From 1820s onwards, much resembling cross-stitch, the beads sewn in rows. From 1860s big beads in tea cosies, firescreens, table mats.

29 Beadwork, detail from 17th-century cushion

Bead-loom work Popular 19th century, for wrist bands and so on (**30**: detail from neck band). Straight-sided flat panels composed wholly of tiny beads and thread without fabric backing (same both sides).

30 Bead-loom work, detail from Victorian neck-band

31 Beaker, silver, 17th century

32 Beilby enamelled decanter and detail of butterfly 'signature'

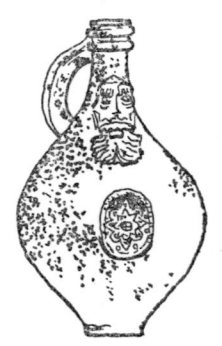

33 Bellarmine

34 Belleek teapot, echinus and coral motif

Bead models Especially 17th century. Beads threaded on wire which was twisted into three-dimensional ornaments such as baskets, flower groups, candlesticks.

Beaker From 16th century. Silver (**31**), pewter, ceramics, horn. Handleless drinking vessel with straight or slightly concave sides tapering inward to the plain base. Many in silver are ornate Victorian-Elizabethan. Through 18th–19th centuries, also in earthenware, white and brown stoneware, at first with silver rims, and bone china.

Bed furniture From medieval days when hung from ceiling. Hangings as distinct from the wooden 'standing bed'. Curtains and corner bonegraces, vallances and corner cantons, bases (below bed frame), coverlets. Great opportunities for embroidery.

Beechwood Little remains pre-18th century, having been subject to worm. Fairly soft, warm light brown, showing small satiny markings when split; good for turnery. To be looked for, unstained, in concealed underframing of over-stuffed furniture. Much cheap furniture, stained, painted or gilded.

Beilby, William and Mary, Newcastle At work from *c.* 1762 (when William 22, his sister 13) to *c.* 1778. Ornament painted in enamels and made permanent in muffle kiln on drinking glasses, decanters (**32**) – heraldic work, rococo scrollwork, trophies, landscapes. Some in colour; some in a dense white. Occasional signature of Beilby or a butterfly motif. Many reproductions.

Bellarmine From 1670s to mid-19th century (and reproductions) copying many imports from Germany. Mottled, brownish. A salt-glazed stoneware full-bellied bottle with handle but no spout (**33**). Narrow neck bearing ugly mask, so that it acquired name of unpopular Cardinal Bellarmine (1542–1621); also sometimes a coat of arms but more often conventional flower motif. Four sizes, gallon to pint.

Belleek porcelain, N. Ireland From 1858. Famous for parian porcelain with iridescent glaze (See *Mother of pearl ware*), some coloured. Many marine motifs (**34**: echinus teapot). Delicate basket work composed of porcelain threads often combined with flower encrustations especially rose, thistle and shamrock. *Ireland* in mark after 1891.

Bellows Ancient, but few now found earlier than 18th century when the wooden boards might be painted, carved, inlaid, japanned or covered with marquetry, beadwork or embroidery. Much Victorian-Elizabethan work.

Bells Especially 18th–19th centuries. Silver: often as inkstand fitting with baluster handle; by 1750s handle might be taper holder or of turned wood or ivory. Glass: 19th century, 9–18 in. tall, various colours with clear clappers. Many modern. Brass: 18th–19th centuries include set (rumblers) composed of several rows of bells under leather hoods worn above the collar by dray horse; Victorian, in fly-terret over horse's head (35).

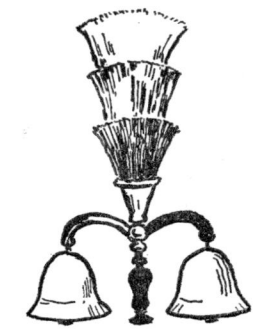

35 Bells on horse's fly terret with coloured horsehair ornament

Bentwood work Ancient process of curving wood by use of steam and heat (shepherds' crooks, hoop-back windsor chairs). More widely applied by English chairmakers from c. 1865, prompted by work of Viennese Thonet brothers. Many light hoop-backed chairs in cheap black-stained wood (36).

Berlin wool work From c. 1805, at first from German patterns; popular 1830s–80s. Embroidery, mainly cross-stitch in worsted wools on squared-mesh canvas, copied from patterns on squared paper. Historical scenes, famous paintings (e.g. Landseer), religious subjects. Also worked in tent stitch, double-cross-stitch, and incorporating chenille, beads. Crude aniline dye-colours from later 1850s. Often mounted on furniture (37: firescreen) or framed as pictures.

36 Bentwood chair

Bevel From 17th century, in mirror glass, the slanting or obtuse-angled border within the frame. Hand-ground at first on very thin glass, wide but too shallow to show prismatic colour.

Bianco-sopra-bianco From 1740s, on tin-enamelled earthenware, especially Bristol. Customary English term (from Italian maiolica) for ornament such as flowers painted in slight relief in white on near-white background (typically starch-blue or lavender-blue) imitating incised or carved Chinese ornament.

Bible box From medieval days but remaining specimens usually 18th or 19th century, often with Victorian or Edwardian amateur carving. Substantial small chest for family records, sometimes including drawer.

37 Berlin wool work on cheval firescreen

38 Biggin coffee pot on heater stand

39 Typical Billie-and-Charlie pendant

40 Bilston painted enamel tea chest containing tea caddies

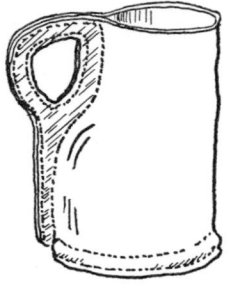

41 Black jack

Biggin, coffee From 1780s. Silver, Sheffield plate. Name from traditional bag-shaped cap worn by young children and for sleeping. Early filter coffee-pot (38). Squat, lidded jug, flat-based for heating and shaped inside to hold a biggin or conical bag of muslin or flannel. Confusing derivation because such vessels made in 1800s by silversmith George Biggin.

Bijouterie Collective term for products of goldsmith and enameller (trinkets such as etui and châtelaine) as distinct from jewellery. Often used also to distinguish personal articles that were carried, such as snuff-box, nutmeg grater, from those that were worn, for which the corresponding word was minuterie (trifles).

Billies and Charlies Second quarter of 19th century. Cheap pewter or lead castings. Pendants (39), medallions, figurines and the like in imagined ancient designs made and 'discovered' in the Thames by William Smith and Charles Eaton. Revealed as fakes by 1858 but now collected.

Billingsley, W. 1760–1828. Brilliant soft-paste porcelain maker – see *Pinxton* (1796–9), *Swansea* (1814–17), *Nantgarw* (1813–14) and (1817–20) – and imaginative flower painter (295). But frequent financial difficulties. Decorator at Worcester (1807–12). At Coalport from 1820.

Bilston enamels Staffordshire. About 1740 to early 19th century. Snuff-boxes, candlesticks, tea chests and caddies (40) and so on. White enamel fused over copper core, variously coloured and hand-painted. Wider range of articles, colours, than *Battersea* (q.v.) Ground colours: dark blue and pea-green from about 1759, turquoise and claret from 1760, rose-pink from 1780s. Late work poor.

Bird call Primitive earthenware. Bird shape with decoy whistle cut in tail.

Bird's eye maplewood Popular in Victorian era for picture and miniature frames. Lustrous golden wood with small dark spots. One of American sugar maples.

Biscuit Porcelain or pottery once fired, porous (not vitrified) before colour or glaze. Derby noted for white biscuit porcelain figures (1773–1830); Bristol (1773–81) for exquisite plaques such as flowers in relief round bust, coat of arms or monogram. Also W. H. Goss, biscuit parian jewellery, later 19th century.

Black jack From 16th century well into 19th. Leather mug **(41)** sometimes silver-mounted and lined with pewter; more cheaply made waterproof with pitch. Jug of similar shape known as bombard.

Blazes 1790s onwards. Glass decoration. Vertical or slanting prismatic cutting (V-cuts to form parallel sharp-angled ridges and hollows) the upper edge in zigzag outline, e.g. around sugar bowl rim or decanter body (**42** : celery glass).

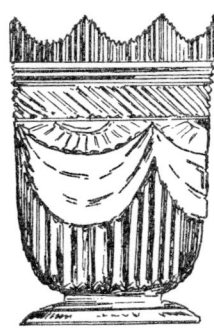

42 Vertical and slanting blazes on Victorian celery glass

Bloor, R. Was proprietor of Derby china factory 1811–1848, following the Duesbury family. Bone china with hard thick glaze. Has caused confusion because 'Bloor-Derby' includes his decorators' hasty, garish ornament on accumulation of earlier (Duesbury) porcelain (mark, **270**).

Blown-moulded glass 1760s–19th century. Vessel shaped by inflating while hot into metal mould **(43)**. Bottles showed dappled surface until 1790s. One-piece moulds to 1802 when two-piece and (1820) three-piece, permitting elaborate surface ornament, with similar undulations inside vessel (in contrast to pressed glass).

Blue-and-white 17th century onwards. Ceramic wares, white surfaced, painted in blue; also, from 1770s, with wear-resistant underglaze blue ornament from printed paper transfers, improved 1780s. Vast trade from 1800s. Blue one of the few heat-resistant colours that could be applied underglaze.

43 Cheap 'tale' glass vessel shaped by blown-moulding

Blue dash charger 17th–18th-century tin-enamelled earthenware plaque, crudely painted, its rim sponge-dabbed to suggest rope work **(44)**. Footrim on back grooved for hanging cord. 20th-century name for much-reproduced work.

44 Blue dash charger

45 Blue glass decanter with gold-lettered 'label'

46 Blue john tazza

47 Bobbin lace (top) contrasted with needlepoint lace

48 Bocage supporting Plymouth figure

Blued steel From *c*. 1768, advertised as new metal. Steel heat-treated against rust, producing oxide colours. For use under friction in high-quality articles, such as snuff and nutmeg rasps.

Blue glass Through 18th–19th centuries at Bristol and eventually at all main glass-making centres such as Sunderland, Newcastle, Stourbridge, Warrington, Waterford. Some of inferior quality from 1800s but good quality, known as smalt glass, from 1820s. Sets of gilt-lettered 'labelled' decanters **(45, 193)**, jugs, tea caddies, scent bottles.

Blue john From *c*. 1750 to present day. Most renowned 1770s–1800. Brittle gemstone fluorspar, amethyst-and-honey tones, mined only in Derbyshire. Main seams soon exhausted. Massive ornamentally-mounted vases followed by smaller wares – tazze **(46)**, pin trays, hand-cooler eggs. Bleu-jaune (blue-yellow) to eager French importers.

Blue tint Glass. Unintentional trace of colour in clear glass, due to impurities such as in Derbyshire lead. Not peculiar to Irish glass. Eliminated by *c*. 1810 (by Blair & Stephenson) but noted in some modern reproductions.

Bobbin lace From 16th century but more in 17th. Pillow lace, created by intertwining threads wound on bobbins. Term often indicating coarse quality, for collars and the like, in heavy threads requiring large bobbins **(47**: typical bobbin ground **(top)** contrasted with simple needlepoint ground).

Bocage From 1760s. Porcelain such as Chelsea, Bow, Derby, Plymouth **(48)**. Support to figure group, important during kiln firing. Tree stump and widespreading branches closely clustered with hand-modelled flowers and leaves. Crude versions in earthenware by *Walton* (q.v.) and others.

Body The basic earthenware, stoneware or other opaque ceramic; for porcelain the equivalent is paste.

Bog wood Ancient oak, yew and other woods preserved in Irish peat bogs. Very dark, suggesting coal. As inlay in 16th–17th centuries. Popular in early Victorian romantic period and conspicuous at Great Exhibition, 1851.

Bombé Furniture line around mid-18th century and Victorian. (French: 'blown out'.)

Swelling outline in, e.g. a commode (49). High quality work requiring immensely skilled veneering. Conspicuous on imported Dutch pieces.

49 *Bombé* outline in mid-Georgian chest of drawers

Bonbonnière 18th century. Silver, Sheffield plate, tortoiseshell, painted enamels (**50**: inverted to open) and so on. Small box for sweets or breath-sweetening comfits. Resembling patch box but without steel mirror. See *Comfit-holders*.

Bone Timeless. Whitish substitute for ivory. Brittle, splintering, its texture lacking the multiplicity of tiny curved lines characteristic of ivory (**226**). Conspicuous in the ship models, games and automata made and sold by French prisoners in England around beginning of 19th century (**343**).

Bone china From 1794. Evolved by Josiah Spode (1733–97). Hard-porcelain ingredients, china clay and china stone strengthened with calcined bone. Brilliantly white, translucent, yet strong and economically practicable, quickly outmoding all soft-paste porcelains.

Bone lace 16th–17th-century name for pillow lace, especially gilt and silver border laces. Rust-proof fish and chicken bones, pared and trimmed, substituted for costly pins while it was worked.

Bone porcelain 1750–75. Soft-paste porcelain strengthened with bone ash. First made at Bow, mainly for dinner and dessert ware; at Chelsea from 1758. Not to be confused with subsequent far more widely manufactured *bone china* (q.v.).

Bonheur du jour From *c.* 1760s; very popular mid-19th century. Lady's slender writing table with drawer and writing slope, the table top fitted with a face-screening section of small drawers, cupboards and shelves (**51**).

Bottle glass curios Mainly 1790s–1840s. Toilet-water flasks, candlesticks, horns,

50 Bonbonnière in painted enamels (detail of opening)

51 *Bonheur du jour*

52 Bottle glass ornaments: horn, walking-stick, pipe

23

53 Bougie box with extinguisher

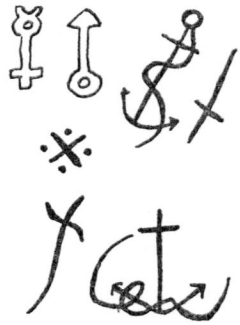

54 Bow marks (two incised, early; the rest, painted, 1760–76)

55 Bracket clock, c. 1700

walking-sticks and similar cheap fairings (**52**), important until high tax was removed from flint-glass, 1845. See *Nailsea glass*.

Bottle tickets See *Wine labels*.

Bouge In a flat vessel, such as a plate, the upward curve between central area and rim.

Bougie box From 17th century (a few); mainly mouse-proof development of *wax-jack* (q.v.) from *c*. 1780s to 1840s. Name from coil of flexible bleached wax taper contained in small round box, its end protruding through tube in lid for use as small, safe light (**53**). Pierced boxes from 1790s, lined with blue glass. Sometimes topped by air-vented gallery holding flint-glass draught shield. Name from Algerian source of candlewax.

Boule (boulle, buhl) Late 17th–19th centuries. Elaborate marquetry for gluing on surface of furniture. Interlacing arabesques cut together from thin sheets of tortoiseshell or horn and brass or silver. Italian process developed by Parisian A. C. Boule (1642–1732) and much reproduced. London-made from 1815.

Boulton, Matthew 1728–1809. Brilliant pioneer of English ormolu (q.v.), some to Adam design. In partnership with John Fothergill from 1762; with James Watt from 1775. All known work now collected – silver, Sheffield plate, cut-steel ornaments and so on.

Bow 1745–76. Soft-paste porcelain comparable with Chelsea. At New Canton factory from 1749 making heavy paste thickly glazed, improved 1755, 1759 (**142, 350**). From *c*. 1765 elaborate table ware, ornaments, figures on scrolling pedestals, including Meissen copies, aided by ex-Chelsea workmen. Ornament, early, in the white and blue-painted Oriental designs, followed by florid colours and final richer brilliance. In 1776 bought by Duesbury and moved to Derby. (**54**: typical marks, two incised, early; others painted, *c*. 1760–76).

Bow front Especially late 18th century. Furniture. Convex or swell front, mainly in chest furniture, succeeding serpentine front.

Bracket clock (or table clock) From later 17th century. Spring driven with short pendulum (introduced 1658). Typically a square front topped by a dome with lifting handle (**55**). Wall bracket for steadiness sometimes made *en suite* with case.

Bracket foot From end of 17th century. In chest or case furniture, roughly triangular support to underframing, extending a few inches each way from the corner and tapering to floor, its edges usually curved and surface frequently waved.

'Brameld' marks on china See *Rockingham*.

Brampton stoneware Mainly 19th century. Brown salt-glazed with close, acid-resistant texture, made near Chesterfield, Derbyshire. Puzzle and hunting jugs (**56**), mugs, loving cups, with relief ornament, some Victorian work bearing 18th-century dates.

56 Brampton hunting jug with greyhound handle

Brass Mainly imported until late 17th century; thereafter increasingly important manufacture (**57**: candlesticks, 18th and 19th centuries). Changes in composition, colour and texture aid dating. Alloy of copper and zinc ore (calamine) until 1770 when might be Emerson's golden-toned alloy of copper and metallic zinc (spelter) – usual from mid-19th century. Solid castings (e.g. candlestick parts) from late 17th century; rolled brass 'raised' (e.g. cooking vessels) from 1730s; machine stamped (e.g. furniture handles) from 1770s; spun hollow ware from late 18th century; complicated single-piece castings in spelter brass from *c.* 1860.

Brazier So named from 17th century. Flat pan for burning charcoal for nearly smokeless warming of room or food.

Breakfront 18th–century case furniture such as bookcase (**58**) with central section of front flanked by wings set slightly forward or back to give an interrupted line.

Bretby ware From 1883. Established by Henry Tooth and William Ault at Woodville, Derbyshire. Extravagantly designed earthenware art pottery such as vases (**59**), some resembling hammered copper, bronze and steel.

57 Brass candlesticks, 18th and 19th centuries

58 Breakfront bookcase, late 18th century

59 Bretby vase with 'wood' finish

25

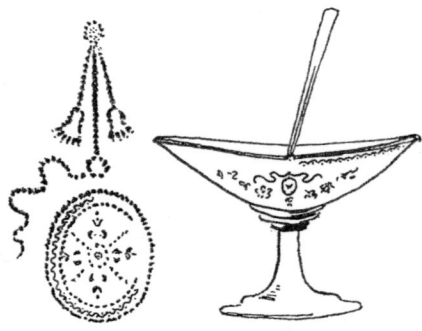

Bright cutting Mainly 1780s–1800s. Silver ornament. Formal borders, swags, engraved with specially shaped gouges to produce faceted effect like delicate chip carving (**60**).

Brisé fan 18th–early 19th centuries. Ivory, fret-cut and/or painted (**61**), mother-of-pearl, tortoiseshell; late specimens very small, sometimes horn, lightly painted bone or very thin laburnum wood; some Victorian in sandal wood. Folding fan composed entirely of sticks and guards without the customary mount, held at perimeter by ribbons.

60 Bright cutting on sugar basket with detail (*left*)

Brislington and Bristol delft About 1640s–late 18th century. Several important factories. White *tin-enamelled ware* (q.v.), harder and denser body than Dutch; thicker, harder white with softer colours than Lambeth or Southwark. Much painting in Chinese style; also heads of royalty and the like, some dated. Effective use of *bianco-sopra-bianco* (q.v.). Plates, punch bowls, brick-shaped flower holders (**62**), tiles and so on.

Bristol glass Mainly late 1740s–1850s. (1) Became renowned for blue, red, green and opaque white or enamel glass. In 1760s Bristol had monopoly of superfine blue for glass-making. 'Bristol blue' now applied also to inferior blue glass irrespective of origin. (2) Enamel glass very white and dense: vases, scent bottles and so on painted like porcelain.

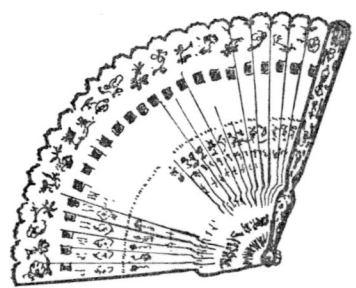

61 *Brisé* fan, painted and fret cut

Bristol porcelain 1748–52 some soft-paste soapstone porcelain. 1770–81 hard-paste porcelain made by W. Cookworthy, previously at Plymouth (see *Plymouth porcelain*). Heat-resistant tea ware, figures, ornaments, shell dishes, sauceboats. Liable to sag, warp, develop fire cracks during manufacture. R. Champion from 1773 (domestic ware, teapots, commissioned services: bright colours, rich gilding. Also now-rare biscuit plaques.) Early mark was chemist's tin symbol; later B with X or numeral up to 8. Champion patent of 1768, extended in modified form, passed to *New Hall* (q.v.).

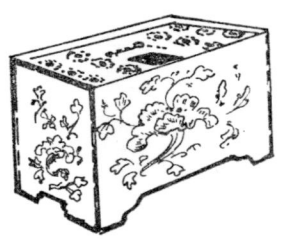

62 Bristol delft, painted and with pierced top for flowers

Bristol pottery Numerous potteries, mainly stoneware. From 1780s good quality cream-coloured earthenware (Temple Backs pottery from 1785), enamel painted and later transfer-printed, especially after 1830. From 1835 brown stoneware became known as Bristol ware when double-dipped in slip glazes by method evolved by W. Powell, Temple Gate pottery, to appear smoothly brown near top of vessel and creamy yellow below.

Bristol stone Rock crystal or colourless quartz found in Clifton limestone. In bijouterie, lockets. Incorrect name for paste jewellery.

Britannia marks on silver plate (1) 1697–1720 and occasionally ever since: indicating *Britannia standard silver* (see below). **(63)**. (2) 1784: with sterling silver marks to indicate exemption of export silver from newly-imposed silver tax, a mark discontinued after seven months.

63 Britannia standard marks (*top*) contrasted with Irish Hibernia mark (18th-century duty mark; later Dublin mark)

Britannia metal 1790s–mid 19th century. Alloy (tin, antimony, copper) like a hard, leadless pewter, silver-bright when new, evolved by *John Vickers* (q.v.). Marked ware by Vickers, James Dixon and others. Domestic wares, teapots and so on, shaped either by die-stamping, including relief ornament, or by spinning, with added cast ornament. In 1820s a little was Sheffield plated; from 1850s some electro-plated. See also *EPBM mark*.

Britannia standard silver Especially 1697–1720. Silver of greater purity (95·8 per cent pure silver) than sterling (92·5 per cent) then obligatory for silver plate, while sterling restricted to coinage. Marked **(63)** with seated figure of Britannia and lion's head erased (wavy neckline). Maker's mark was then first two letters of surname **(218)**. This 'high standard silver' so marked has been optional ever since and liable to misdating.

British plate Patented 1836. Variant of Sheffield plate with similar uses and silver mounts. Very thin silver fused on a whitish nickel alloy instead of on copper. Frequently given pseudo-hallmarks.

64 Typical brocaded Imari pattern on Worcester dish

Brocade 17th–18th century furnishings. Fabric woven with a raised pattern, originally in gold or silver.

Brocaded Imari English name, mid-18th to early 19th century, for export-Japanese (Arita) porcelain with intricate patterns in blue, red and gold and hence to innumerable copies called japans by Worcester **(64)**, Spode, Derby, Mason, Davenport and others.

Broken pediment From beginning of 18th century. On architectural-style furniture – early Georgian mirrors, bookcases **(65)**, clocks. The gabled or arching pediment surmounting the cornice interrupted at the apex by a gap frequently housing a decorative finial.

65 Broken pediment on early Georgian bookcase

66 Bronze powder ornament on papier-mâché paper rack, Wolverhampton style

67 Bulb, carved wood

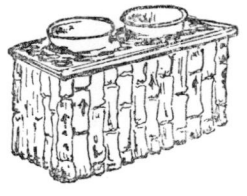

68 Bulb pot (wedgwood bamboo ware)

Bronze Ancient alloy, usually about eight parts copper to one part tin, sometimes with traces of zinc and lead. Enduring cast statuary; medals; bells; costly home equipment such as mortars. For gilded bronze ornament a composition of copper about 80 parts, zinc 20, tin 3, lead 1½ parts.

Bronzes From 18th century. Glittering powders for metallic effects on wood or paper and so on: finely ground from copper, tin and alloys such as brass, heated to widen colour range. Such ornament on papier mâché (**66**: 'Wolverhampton style' on letter rack) patented 1812, popular from 1820s.

Brooks, John At work in London *c.* 1727–60. Dublin engraver, probably largely responsible for development of enormously important technique of *transfer-printing* (q.v.), first on Battersea enamels and subsequently on ceramics.

Buckram Coarse linen or cotton fabric stiffened with gum; backing in upholstery work.

Bulb 16th–early 17th–century ornament. Flemish origin. Massive swelling in turned pillar or leg on bedstead or table, often carved as 'cup and cover'. (**67**). In cheap work composed of several pieces of wood so that leg could be cut from thinner block.

Bulb pots 18th–19th centuries. Ceramics including porcelain, bone china, delft, creamware, fine stonewares (such as jasper), porous terracotta. Vases and covered pots with apertures or rimmed sockets for bulbs or branches (**68**: Wedgwood bamboo ware). Range from mid-Georgian *quintal vases* (q.v.) to Victorian mignonette boxes.

Buncombe, J. Early 19th century. Isle of Wight silhouettist famed among army and navy officers for style of portrait with the uniform painted in brilliant colours and only the eyeless, aristocratic profile in black silhouette. Now reproduced.

Bun foot About 1660s–1720s. From Holland. Flattened ball, popular on chest and desk furniture (**161**).

Bureau From *c.* 1690s. Vague term generally applied to fitted writing desk with slanting front and drawers below.

Burmese glass Late Victorian. Costly, satin-surfaced, semi-opaque, heat-shaded in iridescent tones of deep pink to pale yellow. American patent; made in England by T. Webb & Sons.

Burnishing Rubbing to great brilliance with hard, smooth tool. Possible only on certain types of gilding: on furniture, water gilding; on ceramics, sometimes from 1740s, but more effectively on mercury gilding from 1780s.

Burr wood From 16th century, especially early 18th century, furniture inlay or veneer. Figuring of densely knotted, curled and twisted grain, a growth malformation often found in walnut, yew, elm, maple, alder.

Butler's tray From *c.* 1720s, but more in late 18th–19th centuries. Large rectangular tray with hand holes in vertical rim, accompanied by folding stand of wood and webbing. Mahogany, good quality to withstand staining. For the butler to bring in and officiate over his equipment of bottles and glasses (**69**, which also shows so-called coach table variant).

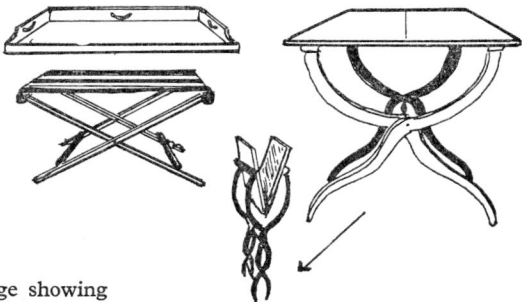

Butt hinge Cupboard door hinge showing only thin line of metal. Far the most usual type on high quality antique furniture but often replaced by more showy designs.

69 Butlers' trays: with webbing supporting loose tray and with folding wooden top

Butterfly table 18th–19th centuries. Light table with hinged flaps supported by hinged arms instead of gate-legs, these, from their shape, known as butterfly or fly brackets.

Buttoning From second half of 18th century, for upholstery work, known as quilting. More pronounced in Victorian use.

Buttons From mid-16th century, jewelled gold; from end-16th-century silver, brass, tin. Hallmark on back from 1720, so that they became more popular. Various 18th–19th-century laws controlling manufacture in different materials. Dating aided by changes in shaping methods and shank attachment.

70 Cabochon from carver's 1760s trade card

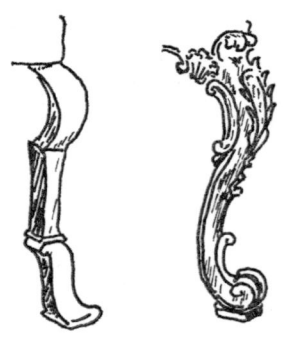

71 Cabriole legs, Queen Anne (*left*) and George II

72 Caddy ladles, tea-leaf shape and with fiddle handle

Cabaret set From mid-18th century. Ceramics. One-person or two-person tea-set, including matching ceramic tray.

Cabinet-maker From 17th century. Craftsman trained in refinements of furniture construction, such as veneering, beyond range of joiner.

Cabochon ornament From 16th century as round or oval swelling among strapwork (like smooth, unfaceted jewel); in 18th century surrounded by formalised acanthus leaves, popular in association with shell on early Georgian cabriole leg (70).

Cabriole leg Mainly *c.* 1700–50. Derived from classic design, early specimens suggesting animal's leg. Tapering leg, somewhat S-curved, rounded out at the knee and in at the ankle above a hoof, paw, club or other projecting foot (71: Queen Anne and George II specimens).

Cabriolet fan *c.* 1755, from France. The mount formed of two or three narrow arc-shaped bands, the widest, at top, painted with scene featuring the then-fashionable two-wheel carriage (162).

Caddy ladle Mainly from *c.* 1770s. Usually silver. Short-handled scoop for measuring dry tea leaves into teapot. Many decorative shapes including early shell, fruiting vine of 1790s–1800s, cupped hand, tea leaf (72). Some fiddle-shaped handles from *c.* 1800.

Cameo Stone, shell, ceramics, glass. Ornament fashioned in relief against background of contrasting tone; e.g. Wedgwood late 18th-century jasper ware; Minton pâte-sur-pâte *c.* 1870; cameo glass (73).

Cameo glass 1851 prize offered by the Richardson glass manufacturers to reproduce

Portland vase (q.v.) led to carving of vessels in *cased glass* (q.v.) light over dark, like layered stone. Important work by John Northwood such as classical figure designs and by George and Thomas Woodall. Commercial work by 1880s, mainly floral (**73**), some aided by engraving wheels and hydrofluoric acid. Cheaper imitations in *etched glass* (q.v.).

Candelabrum Fashionable from 18th century. Branched candlestick holding two or more candles (**74, 297**).

Cane furniture From 1660s. Split cane formed into open mesh. Coarse at first but finer towards 1700. Introduced as light, resilient seats and back panels in 'Charles II' chair (**363**) and daybed. Soon out of fashion in 18th century but favoured again towards 1800 (**75**: from Sheraton's Encyclopaedia).

Cane-ware From *c.* 1770, evolved by Wedgwood. Fine-stoneware in creamy-buff tones. Fireproof variant from 1850s used for baking dishes.

Canterbury Furniture. Late 18th–century mobile stand with vertical partitions (**20**). Sheraton, 1803, noted the term then in use both for a music stand and for a fitted supper trolley.

Carat Measure of fineness of gold, pure gold being 24 carat. Hallmarks aid dating. Until 1798 standard was 22 carat (22 parts gold to 2 parts alloy – copper – for wear-resistance, as in sovereign). Hallmarked like silver until 1844. Act of 1798 legalised lower standard of 18 carat with hallmark of crown and figure 18. Act of 1854 permitted also 15, 12 and 9 carat, with figures included in hallmarks. In 1932 14 carat replaced 15 and 12 carat standards. In 19th-century colour of alloyed gold controlled by inclusion of silver and zinc as well as copper. Alloy sometimes removed chemically from surface which, until worn, was then radiant pure gold.

Card case Engraved visiting cards by mid-18th century but remaining cases usually 19th century: silver (engraved, engine-turned, press embossed), carved ivory, mother of pearl and/or tortoiseshell (**470**), lacquered wood, papier mâché, Tunbridge ware, tooled leather, flower-painted bone china, sandalwood, cross-stitch embroidery, painted wood with Scottish views and tartan grounds. Usually about $4 \times 3 \times \frac{7}{16}$ in. with deep lid sliding off or hinged on narrow side; occasionally book-shaped or other more elaborate design (**76**).

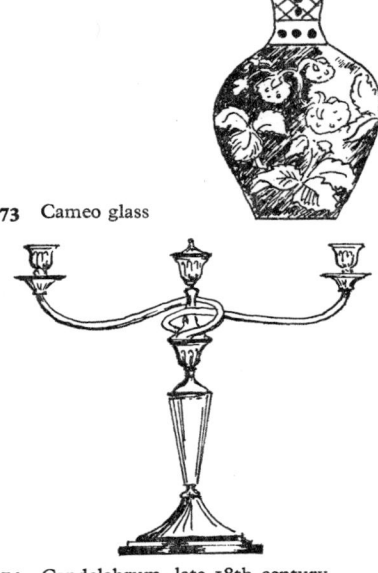

73 Cameo glass

74 Candelabrum, late 18th century

75 Cane-backed chair from Sheraton's *Encyclopaedia*

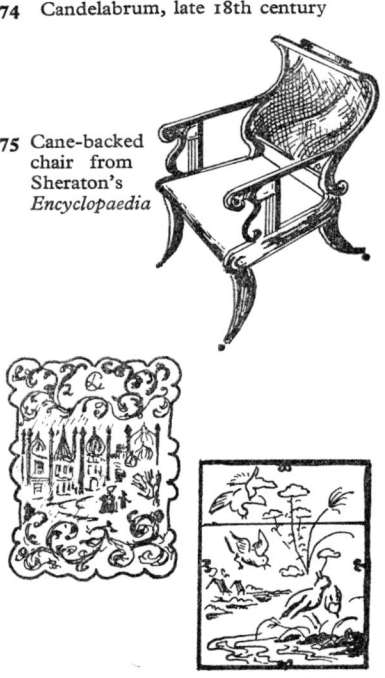

76 Card cases: silver, 1841 (Brighton Pavilion) and ivory, gilded

31

77 Card-cut strengthening applied to silver jug

78 Cartouche from early Georgian bookcase cresting

79 Cased glass perfume bottle (ornament ground through red and white to clear glass)

80 Cast iron: Doyle's Mr Punch as door porter

Card-cut ornament Furniture. Lattice ornament, carved in shallow relief or pierced and applied, on friezes, chairs and so on, especially on mid-18th–century 'Chinese' furniture. Similar effect to strengthen some early 18th–century silver (**77**).

Carolean, Caroline Relating to fashions current in reigns of Charles I (1625–49) and Charles II (1660–85), especially the latter.

Cartouche. Furniture (**78**), metal work. Ornament in style of informal escutcheon with central space for crest or cypher surrounded by 'unrolled' scrolls, often asymmetrical.

Caryatid Furniture, especially around 1600 and 1800 and mid-Victorian. From classical architecture. Female figure carved in relief, used as pilaster or corner support on cupboard, bed, desk. Male equivalent is Atlantis.

Cased glass 19th century, especially from 1845. Two or more layers of glass in different colours fused together and usually blown into hollow ware. Pattern achieved by oblique grinding through outer layers of this overlay to reveal innermost colour rimmed with intervening colours (**79**).

Casting, ceramics From 1730s. Unfired earthenware in the liquid form of slip poured into a porous plaster mould, revolved for even distribution and the rest poured away again as soon as a crust of sufficient thickness has formed against the mould surfaces.

Casting, metal Molten silver, pewter, brass, copper, shaped by pouring into mould to cool. In later 18th century largely replaced by cheaper rolling and die-stamping, the hollow back made solid with a cheap filling. See also *cire perdue*.

Cast iron Probably from 15th century for *firebacks* (q.v.) and so on, including much 19th-century furniture. Hard and cheap for repetitive work but brittle, in contrast to wrought iron (**80**: familiar Doyle Punch as door porter).

Castleford ware *c.* 1795–1821. Under D. Dunderdale made cream-ware, black basaltes, tortoiseshell ware and relief-patterned vitrified stoneware. Remembered for style of moulded teapots then made by several firms with hinged or sliding lids **(81)**, possibly chess sets (unmarked and much reproduction work).

81 Castleford relief-patterned teapot

Castle Hedingham pottery 1864–1901. Bingham family. 'Primitive' style and ornament, sometimes including misleading 17th-century dates. Popular 'Essex' jug **(82)** commemorates Boadicea's victory over Romans and Dunmow flitch procession, with hops, wheat and oysters, also arms of Essex boroughs and ancient Essex families.

Castors From early 18th century. Small solid wheels for furniture. Hard wood followed by broad rollers composed of leather discs between brass arms. From *c.* 1770 wholly of brass. By Regency period many designs including brass sockets for projecting feet. Glazed earthenware from 1851.

82 Castle Hedingham jug with applied motifs relating to Essex history

Caughley *c.* 1775–99. Salopian China Manufactory, Shropshire, under Thomas Turner. Useful wares in soft-paste soapstone porcelain much like Worcester, mainly painted or printed in blue, the patterns including pseudo-Oriental Fisherman **(83**: smaller fish than Worcester), Willow, Broseley-dragon. Marks included *C* and *S* in blue and SALOPIAN impressed.

Cauldron Spherical pot with swing handle and often three legs for use on primitive down-hearth. In medieval bronze and iron; in copper and hammered brass from *c.* 1580s. Still being made in late 19th century.

83 Caughley porcelain version of familiar Fisherman pattern

Cauliflower ware From *c.* 1755. Developed by Wedgwood and Whieldon in partnership. Cream-coloured earthenware relief-modelled and glaze-coloured to suggest cauliflowers, pineapples **(84)**, sweetcorn. Tea-ware, punch pots and so on. Many 19th–century reproductions in inferior colours.

Cellaret See *Wine waiter*.

Celluloid 1855 patented by Parkes of Birmingham. Forerunner of transparent plastics.

Chafing dish From medieval days, small portable metal grate (chafing stand) to hold refined smokeless charcoal for warming food in accompanying dish. From late 18th and through 19th centuries, a silver-lidded dish on

84 Pineapple mould-patterned jug in cauliflower ware

85 Chamber candlestick in electro-plate for 1851 Exhibition

stand with spirit lamp; hot water compartment beneath dish kept food from burning.

Chamber candlestick From 17th century. Silver, brass, ceramics. For carrying from room to room. Candle socket mounted on drip-catching saucer with scroll or loop handle (**85:** electro-plate, 1851). Sometimes slot in base of socket for snuffers and handle slot for peg of chain-secured cone extinguisher.

Chamberlain, Worcester About 1783–1852. Robert Chamberlain, trained at Worcester porcelain factory, became independent porcelain decorator and, from 1790s, manufacturer of bone china (**314, 520**); also, from 1811, of costly 'Regent china'. In 1840 acquired older *Worcester* company (q.v.). Noted for magnificent painted ornaments, dinner wares, fluted tea wares.

Chamfered corner Furniture. Canted surface produced by bevelling off an angle edge. On many 18th–century tallboys, corner cupboards (**86**) and so on.

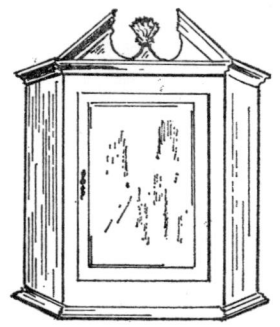

86 Chamfered corners on hanging corner cupboard

Chandelier Medieval term in common 18th–century use for pendant fitting to provide overhead light from a number of candles. Costly early specimens silver, rock crystal and so on; some late 17th–century brass; became important in Georgian glass which may be dated by styles of cut ornament.

Chantilly sprig On 18th–century English porcelain, popular cornflower-and-forget-me-not motif copied from French (**87**).

Chapter ring Brass; sometimes silver or silvered. Ring on clock dial engraved with hours and minutes.

'Charlotte at the Tomb of Werther' Late 18th century to early Victorian. Painted ornament, embroidery, jewellery and so on. Grief-stricken figure at urn-topped tomb among weeping willows. Widely popular ornament associated with Goethe's novel *The Sorrows of Young Werther*.

Chasing Ornament of metals, especially silver, with hammer and punches which push the metal from the back into highly embossed (repoussé) or very low relief. Detail may be sharpened by further punchwork (flat chasing) on front but, in contrast to engraving, no metal is cut away.

87 Chantilly sprig motif on English porcelain

Cheese toaster From about 1770. Silver, Sheffield plate (**88**). Oblong lidded serving

34

dish containing set of individual dishes over hot water compartment, filled through aperture in projecting handle at back. Hinged lid linked to handle by adjustable chain. When thrust towards fire the partly open lid reflected heat on to cheese snacks lying flat in the dishes.

Chelsea porcelain About 1743–56 and 1758–69. Finest English soft-paste porcelain. Periods now known by marks (**90**: in sequence) although much unmarked and many mark forgeries. Incised triangle mark, 1743–7 (not to be confused with some 19th–century triangle marks): mainly table ware, much adapted from silver designs and with ornament in relief. Raised anchor mark, 1747–55: table ware and a few figures including fine birds. Improving paste with thick creamy glaze. Red anchor (occasionally blue or purple), 1753–6: thinner, more translucent paste, smooth glaze, sharp modelling including applied flowers picked out in pastel colours. Gold anchor, 1758–69: denser paste with soft limpid glaze, liable to firecracks and crazing, but fine figure modelling (**89**), wonderful ground colours (mazarine blue, pea-green, 1759; claret, turquoise, 1760; yellow, 1761) heavily enriched with gold. Oriental, Meissen and Sèvres influences, with increasing use of colour and gold. See also *Sprimont*.

Chelsea-Derby 1770–84. Chelsea productions under ownership of Derby's William Duesbury, with smooth, waxy porcelain in Sèvres style. Cheaper red instead of costly ground colours. Table ware, Boucher-style figures and so on, marked with Chelsea gold anchor traversing down-stroke of script D, with jewelled crown above from 1773, (**90**: two marks).

88 Cheese toaster, the lid held open to reflect heat on to the dishes

89 Chelsea porcelain shepherdess

90 Chelsea and Chelsea-Derby. Five Chelsea marks including incised triangle and raised anchor, with two Chelsea-Derby marks below

35

91 Chess pieces (king and pawn) in hard-stone, *c.* 1800

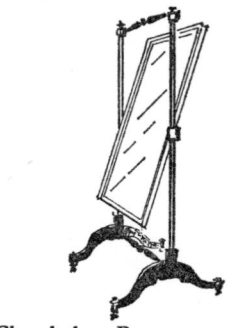

92 Cheval glass, Regency

93 Chimney furniture: dog grate, late 18th century

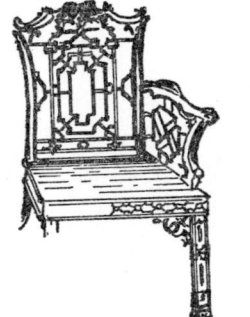

94 'Chinese' furniture: Chippendale *Director* chair design

Chessmen Distinctly graded from 12th century. Early in ivory, bone, hardwood. Precious metals and jewelled from late 17th century; cheap sets in bronze and pewter until Victorian days. English sets in carved ivory from 1740s, horn, amber, agate, glass, hard-stone (**91**: *c.* 1800), ceramics, including Doulton and Wedgwood. See also *Staunton chess set.*

Cheval furniture 19th–century term for what 18th century knew as horse furniture. Firescreens (**37**); Regency and later dressing glasses (**92, 359**). Screen or mirror flanked by two vertical supports in inverted T shape, each on forward-and-backward-projecting foot and linked by low stretcher.

Chicken skin Most delicate pliant variety of lambskin vellum used as mounts on highest quality hand-painted folding fans.

Chiffonier Mainly from early 19th century. In England a low cupboard with drawers, sometimes topped and flanked by small open shelves. Confusing, because this in French is a chiffonière, whereas a French chiffonier can be a tall cupboard.

Chimney furniture Includes iron *firebacks* (q.v.), firedogs and creepers for log down-hearth, grates for wood and coal (**93**: late 18th–century dog grate) fenders and such tools as tongs, shovels, bellows; also kitchen *crane, spit, spit-jack, spit-rack* and *trivet* (qq.v).

Chimney ornaments 19th century. Ceramics, brass and other metals, coloured glass. Term mainly applied to small cheap celebrity figures, miniature furniture, shoes and the like for mantelpiece, especially the *flat-back figure* (q.v.).

China Originally the vitreous, translucent, 'hard' *porcelain* (q.v.) imported from China. Now generally applied to glazed ceramic wares ranging from translucent bone china to earthenwares such as ironstone china and stone china.

'Chinese' furniture Especially mid-18th and early 19th centuries. Taste stimulated by Oriental imports from 1660s, expressed in minor japanned furniture of early 18th century and more substantial chairs, tables, cabinets, basically European but often in distinctively square outlines and with Chinese fret ornament (**94**: Chippendale design).

'Chinese Lowestoft' See *Lowestoft*.

Chinoiserie From 17th century. General term for European notions of Oriental design and ornament, e.g. silver tea caddies with repoussé figures of Chinamen **(95)** and ceramics with such blue painted or printed patterns as Willow **(508)** and Fisherman **(83)**. (**96**: furniture detail from Chippendale's 'Chinese sopha' design).

95 Chinoiserie ornament in repoussé work on silver tea caddy

Chintz From 17th century. Introduced from India as dye-patterned white cotton cloths. Use restricted in deference to English woollen industry. Imitated in England from late 17th century on linen and cotton by block-printing with fast dyes. Included notable 18th–century monochrome pictorial printing from copper plates (England 20 years ahead of now-famous French toiles de Jouy). Roller-printing from 1780s.

Chippendale family Thomas (1719–79) operated cabinet makers' and upholsterers' business – eventually also general house furnishers – in London from *c.* 1748, continued by son until 1822.

Chippendale furniture Widely made by his contemporaries, comparable with the fashionable designs **(94, 96, 192, 364, 476)** recorded in his catalogue *The Gentleman and Cabinet-Maker's Director* (1754, 1755, 1762). Important work that can be ascribed to his firm is in the subsequent contrasting neo-classic style.

96 Chinoiserie detail from Chippendale 'Chinese sopha' design

Chocolate pot From late 17th century, mainly 18th **(97)**. Silver, etc. Distinguishable from coffee-pot when it had a small lidded aperture in top of cover for a boxwood mill or swizzle stick to froth up the thick liquid before pouring. (Notched knop at end of slender handle, whirled between one's hands.)

Christmas card Egley's famous 1842 design followed by a few on general sale from 1846 but mainly from 1860s. Coloured lithographs; frosted from 1867; religious from late 1860s; three-dimensional and trick in 1880s; booklets from 1884; fringed from 1889; crude jokes in 1890s.

97 Chocolate pot with hinged lid to swizzle stick aperture, early 18th century

Chromolithograph From c. 1840, as costly, greatly admired coloured print produced by printing on paper in different colours from three or four lithographic stones in succession (later often zinc or aluminium). From 1870s development of lithographic printing machine transformed it largely into cheap commercial process for Christmas cards and the like.

Cire perdue casting Ancient method for casting intricate shapes in metals. Moulding sand was packed closely round the model which, being wax, was then melted and poured away (lost) and the space filled with molten metal.

Clay, Henry inventor of highly successful *paper-ware* (q.v.) patented 1772 and made for 100 years – a superior form of later pressed papier mâché.

Close nailing From 16th century. Brass-headed nails in closely spaced rows or pattern attaching hide, haircloth and similar inelastic materials used for chairs and to water-proof travelling coffers.

Close plating Ancient process of sealing silver leaf to surface of base metal. Impermanent 'French plating' from early 18th century on brass and copper. English patent 1779 especially for edged and pointed steel cutlery tools to avoid tainting from acid foods. Improved method 1809 using silver foil. Some marked from 1806.

Club foot From c. 1705. Rounded projection like head of club, simplest style of foot for a cabriole leg (e.g. **100**).

Coaching inn clock From 1740s. Wall timepiece (no striking mechanism), weight driven, with large unglazed face for maximum visibility and short body, especially for coaching inns where time schedule important (**98**). Often known as Act of Parliament clock because its popularity wrongly attributed to Pitt's extremely brief 1797 tax on watches and clocks.

Coade stone Late 18th century (Lambeth) to 1830s. Artificial stone like terracotta was used architecturally and for garden ornaments, vases, sculpture work because frost-resistant. Name from owner of process, Mrs. Eleanor Coade.

Coal Can be confusing in early records which refer to charcoal prepared by skilled smouldering of wood to obtain hot, smokeless

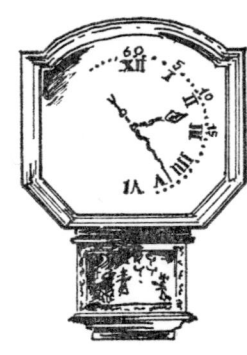

98 Coaching inn clock (black japanned with gilded ornament)

fuel (best quality known as court charcoal). Mined coal was 'sea coal' because mainly transported by ship.

Coalport Shropshire. About 1795–1926; then at Stoke-on-Trent. Until 1841 under John Rose who bought out Caughley factory. Some hard porcelain resembling New Hall, then bone china of improving quality and some feldspar porcelain. Leadless glaze introduced 1820. Very rich style and ornament from 1830s **(99)**. Marks include COLEBROOK DALE, CD, CSN in ampersand. The date A.D. 1750 in several marks used from 1875.

Coaster See *Wine coaster*.

Cock beading From *c.* 1730, customary on mahogany. Small beading projecting outwards around edge of drawer.

Cockfighting chair From *c.* 1730s. Misleading name for conversation or reading chair for a man to sit astride, back-to-front, without creasing his coat-tails. Arm rest instead of back cresting and this may be elaborated to contain folding bookrest, candle stand **(100)**.

Cockshead hinge From 16th century on cupboards. Variant of H hinge, with each arm an elongated S with foliate end **(101)**. Wrought iron, thinning towards extremities and with bevelled edges. Often reproduced.

Coffer Weather-resistant chest with rounded top, leather or cloth covered (close nailed), often banded with metal for valuables. Coffered panel: sunk panel as opposed to projecting or fielded panel.

Coloured glass From *c.* 1720s, some high quality blue, followed by green, red and amethyst flint-glass; from *c.* 1790, low-taxed, brownish-green bottle glass with surface flecks and mottling (so-called *Nailsea*, q.v.); from *c.* 1800, pale green bottle glass coloured semi-opaque blue, green, amber, red for surface ornament; from 1845, on tax abolition, full range of colour in flint-glass **(45, 79)**.

Coloured prints Either hand-coloured (may be recent addition) or printed in colour as in some 18th–19th century wood-block prints, stipple engravings (when the dots carry the colour) and 19th–century chromolithographs. See also *Baxter prints* and *Le Blond prints*.

Combed ware Earthenware ornament. Viscid clay-and-water slips, in contrasting

99 Coalport: lidded *pot-pourri* vase, flower encrusted

100 'Cockfighting' conversation chair, early Georgian

101 Cockshead hinge (iron)

39

102 Commemorative jug with crude portrait of Wellington

103 Commode with serpentine top, ormolu corner ornaments

104 Console table, *c.* 1750

tones, applied to surface and worked into parallel wavy lines with a toothed tool, suggesting paper marbling.

Comfit-holders 18th–19th centuries. Ceramics, glass. Decorative small vessels prominent at informal social gatherings for guests to help themselves to breath-sweetening comfits – tiny strongly scented sweets (popular from 15th century). Thus a pair of porcelain figures might offer baskets of aniseed balls for the gentlemen, violet cachous for the ladies. *Bonbonnières* (q.v.) for pocket use.

Commemorative wares Plates, jugs, mugs, busts issued as souvenirs for important occasions (**102**: Wellington jug, moulded and painted). Confusing when celebrating centenaries and the like; e.g. Shakespeare's birth (1564) widely commemorated in 1864; Trafalgar in 1905; Columbus in 1906; Charles Dickens (50 years after death) 1920.

Commode From 1750s highly fashionable as a low, footed chest for drawing room, with ornate marquetry (**297**), japanning, inlay or carving on a front composed of door panels (**103**) or drawers. Frequently in bombé, serpentine outline; bow fronted *c.* 1790s. Term for bedroom cupboard only from Victorian days.

Compendium Specimens remain from 17th century. Most elaborate in early 19th century. Box or casket handsomely fitted for the toilet, writing, needlework (**226**), jewellery, hobbies. Some for men.

Console table From 1700s. Ornate table with a wall bracket (console) instead of back legs, so as to fit close against a dadoed wall, usually under a mirror (**104**).

Copeland china William Copeland joined Josiah Spode (q.v.) in 1797 and in 1829 his son, W. T. Copeland, became proprietor, followed by direct descendants ever since. Marks (**105**) include several incorporating name *Spode* (q.v.).

Copper lustre From *c.* 1790s. Earthenware or china covered or patterned with extremely thin iridescent metal applied in solution and fired in muffle-kiln. Range of tones obtained from copper-alloyed gold, often on reddish clay ground after 1823. From mid-1820s copper oxide used on heavy, inferior ware (**106**). Reproductions abound. From late 1880s Doulton copper lustre on silicon stoneware including imitation seams and rivets.

105 Copeland china marks

Copper ware Mainly 19th century. Jelly moulds, pans, urns. Some heavy jugs, warming pans **(494)**, in rolled copper sheet from *c.* 1730s; articles such as cooking pots, drop-stamped from *c.* 1780s; spun hollow-ware from *c.* 1820.

Cordial glass 18th century. Small bowled glass for strongly alcoholic drink served with evening tea and therefore ornate to go with porcelain. Pre-1740, thick-walled funnel or bell bowl; post-1740, engraved or lightly cut bucket or trumpet bowl with twist or facet-cut stem **(107**: specimens of 1740s–1760s).

Corkscrew From 16th century auger type known as wimble; pointed helix spiral forged from steel wire from mid-17th century: often fluted screw from *c.* 1780. Sheathed pocket style from *c.* 1750; screw with cylindrical socket for bottle top – 'the king's screw' – patented 1794 and other patents followed **(108**: pocket styles, *c.* 1800).

Corner chair From *c.* 1730s popular for cards, writing-table, because looked well from back view. Four equidistant legs with especially handsome cabriole for centre front. Low rounded cresting rail with three vertical supports and two intervening splats.

Costrel Silver, ceramics. Ancient form of pilgrim's or traveller's bottle shaped as flattened globe with shoulder loops for carrying strap. Popular shape for Victorian ornaments. Many modern copies.

Cottages Also castles, summer-houses and so on. Ceramic, especially early 19th–century bone china **(109)**. Frequently has back aperture or lifts off base for inserting sweetly-scented smouldering pastille or slow-burning nightlight (hollow chimney or cut-out

106 Copper lustre serving jug, early Victorian

107 Cordial glasses in successive styles, 1740–60s

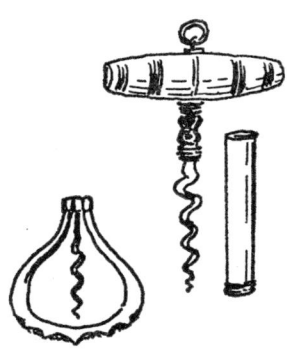

108 Corkscrews, pocket designs, *c.* 1800

109 Cottage pastille burner, bone china

110 Court cupboard, 17th century

111 Cow with milkmaid, earthenware, early 19th century

112 Crabstock handle and spout, *c.* 1750s

windows). Many modern reproductions. See also *Pastille burner.*

Counters (games) From 17th century, thin discs of ivory, tortoiseshell, stained bone, brass, pewter. Throughout 18th century especially mother-of-pearl lightly carved or engraved, including rectangles and fish shapes. From *c.* 1850 gilt-metal 'coins' such as guineas made in vast numbers until replicas prohibited in 1862.

Court cupboard 16th–17th–century side table for serving drinks during meal in space-saving short (court) design of two or three tiers supported on corner pillars **(110)**.

Cow jug Silver (*c.* 1755) with open mouth; filled through lidded hole in back. Widely imitated as earthenware ornament in early 19th century, cheaply hand-coloured (orange, green, yellow, dull blue), mottled with lustre, or transfer-printed. Sometimes with tiny milkmaid **(111)**.

Crabstock handle Ceramics. Easy-to-grip handle on jug, mug, teapot, shaped like gnarled branch of crab-apple **(112)**.

Cradle Furniture. Child's bed on rockers as distinct from swinging form on end supports (cot) and four-legged spindle-surrounded crib. Found from 17th century in wood; later 18th century cane; 19th century wrought iron, always with osier as cheaper alternative.

Cradle, ceramic From 17th century in slipware, as new-baby gift, sometimes with initials and date. From *c.* 1750s into Victorian days, in wide range of earthenwares as 'wrapping' for congratulatory gift.

Crane Wrought-iron bracket for suspending cooking-pots over fire, shaped for pot hooks and often adjustable both horizontally and vertically to make full use of fire.

Crayon engraving Popular late 18th-century style of etching, the copper plate stippled with roulettes to suggest grained lines of chalk drawing on rough paper. Frequently in red, warm brown or bistre tone. Not to be confused with the 'soft pencil' lines of soft ground etchings and many early 19th-century lithographs.

Crazing Ceramics. Tiny hair-line cracks caused when imperfectly matched ware and glaze responded differently to atmospheric changes. Also on japanned furniture. Fake crazing tends to be coarser. As deliberate ornament is known as crackle.

Creamware Cream-coloured earthenware. Vastly successful refined earthenware dipped in liquid glaze. Evolved 1740s and greatly improved by Wedgwood in 1760s (queen's ware) and again 1776. Made largely also by Leeds from 1760s, and throughout Potteries.

Creepers In primitive down-hearth small firedogs to support firewood while larger ones flanking them were kept bright for show.

Crewel work Especially later 17th century. Embroidery on linen hangings, cushion covers and so on. Many expansive foliage patterns in fascinating range of stitches (113). Crewels were cheap to buy, being the ends of worsted cut from the loom by the weaver.

Crime piece mantel ornaments Named pottery models of buildings once popular for association with early 19th–century murders. Include Polstead Red Barn (1828), Potash Farm (114) and Stanfield Hall (1848).

Crizzling Permanent defect in imperfectly manufactured glass vessels such as much 17th-century flint-glass, which in course of months or years became opaque.

Cross-stitch embroidery From 16th century but associated especially with early Victorian Berlin wool work. Two-stitch Xs in regular rows on meshed double-thread canvas (115 top). Also known as gros-point and tapestry stitch, but should not be called *tapestry* (q.v.).

Crown Derby china Derby porcelain mark might include a crown from *c.* 1773, but the Derby Crown Porcelain Co. was founded 1877. See also *Derby*.

Crowned X pewter From 1750s this mark designated a fine hard pewter. (From 1697 Pewterers' Company allowed an X mark on 'extraordinary ware'.)

Crown glass For cabinet work. Blown, then flattened by spinning; thinner from 1740s – hence great improvement in cabinets. Distorted centre known as bull's eye.

Crystal Modern term for fine flint-glass.

Crystal cameo 1819–35, made by *Apsley Pellatt* (q.v.). 1845–65, less perfect copies by other glassmen. Small bas-relief celebrity

113 Crewel work detail from curtain

114 Crime piece: pottery model of Potash Farm, Cornish home of murderer James Rush

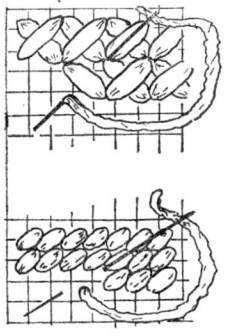

115 Cross-stitch (*above*) and tent-stitch

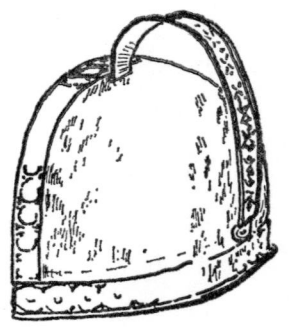

116 Curfew, brass

117 Cut steel detail from châtelaine, 1851

portrait or other motif cast in china clay and wholly enclosed in extremely clear flint-glass. Some vividly coloured coats of arms. Found as paper weights, toilet bottles, mugs and other vessels. Often termed sulphides; Pellatt called them crystallo-ceramics.

Curfew From medieval times, method of complying with edict that household fires had to be put out or covered at night. Quarter-sphere of heavy iron, brass (**116**) or copper, fitting close against fireback. Now rare.

Cut steel 1760s–1860s, in deteriorating qualities. Ornament on boxes, fan-sticks, reticules, buttons, buckles. Early facet-cut 'gems' of wrought steel, hand forged and claw mounted. From *c.* 1765, factory-made 'gems' riveted to cast steel mounts. From early 1840s, facets stamped *en bloc* (**117**: detail of 1851 châtelaine).

Cwpwrdd deudarn and tridarn From late 17th century. Welsh versions of massive hall or parlour cupboard with upper tier of smaller cupboards above main storage. Tridarn has additional topmost tier as a hooded canopy for display-china.

Cylinder fall desk From late 18th century. Fitted desk with quarter-circle lid opening back into body of bureau. Solid, not slatted (see *Tambour*), usually veneered mahogany.

118 Dates in ceramic marks: Coalport, late 19th century and Mortlock, 1880s

Daguerreotype From 1839. Early form of photograph.

Damascening Ancient style of arabesque ornament with gold or silver wire hammered into grooves undercut into metal surfaces, such as weapons. Not much English work.

Date letter on silver Single letter in punch outline among the row of hallmarks. To interpret, one must identify another mark which indicates where silver was assayed, such as anchor mark of Birmingham. Each assay office used its own list of letters, changed annually.

Date symbols on china A few firms introduced year symbols which aid dating: e.g. Minton from 1842, Wedgwood from 1860, Worcester from 1867.

Dates in ceramic marks Often misleading since they refer to the year of a factory's establishment. Much mid-Victorian use (**118**: Coalport and Mortlock). See *Coalport*.

Dates in furniture carving Dangerous to beginner. Popular in 17th century and therefore widely found on Victorian work – black oak sideboards and the like.

Davenport china 1793–1882, at Longport. John Davenport established high reputation for earthenware, bone china (**119**), stone china. Products ranged from magnificent japanned ornament to piecrust ware. Also glass in early 19th century.

Davenport Furniture. From end of 18th century; more from *c.* 1830. Small chest of drawers topped by sloping desk, mainly for lady's use. Drawers open to one side, matched by sham drawer fronts on opposite side (**120**: Regency). Victorian specimens often heavily scrolled below desk section.

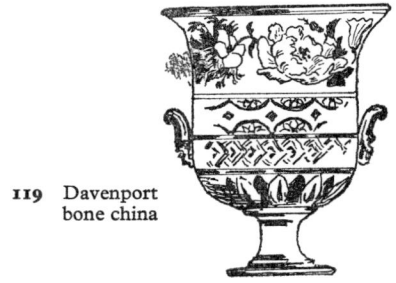

119 Davenport bone china

120 Davenport desk, Regency

45

121–122 Glass decanters: Prussian shape, *c.* 1800 (*left*) and deep diamond cutting, 1851

Deal From German for sawn timber: hence planks of softwood such as pine and fir largely imported from Baltic countries for use in out-of-sight furniture carcase work and in painted panelling.

Decanter From late 17th century. Stoppered glass vessel for tabling wine. Mallet shape, 1700–30, quatrefoil, 1730s–60s; shouldered, *c.* 1740s–60s; with painted label **(45)**, 1755–80 and 1810–20; champagne (with ice pocket), from 1750s; taper, 1765–1800s; barrel **(25)**, 1775–1800s; prussian, 1775–1830 **(121**: *c.* 1800); cylindrical, 1790s–1830s. Heavy cut ornament mainly from 1800s **(122**: by Richardson, 1851).

Delany, Mrs. Mary Granville (1700–88), niece of Lord Lansdown. Second marriage, 1743, was to Dr. Patrick Delany, Dean of Down (d. 1768). Friend of royalty and frequent visitor to Duchess of Portland. Many detailed letters quoted by her biographer, grand-niece Lady Llanover. Despite full society life and eventual failing sight, she copied 72 famous paintings, studied literature, astronomy, mineralogy, music, designed and worked embroideries for bed hangings, dress, and shared period's delight in such hobbies as collecting exotic shells and amateur turnery. See also *Paper mosaics*.

Delft ware See *Tin-enamelled ware*.

Della Robbia ware 1894–1906. Briefly successful art pottery at Birkenhead founded by artist-trained Henry Rathbone. Earthenware architectural ornament such as relief-modelled figure panels; also wall plaques, plates, vases with opaque white grounds as basis for patterns in incised lines and flowing colours. Two artists might sign initials, one for the pattern lines, the other for the colour.

De Morgan, William 1839–1917. From 1872, decorator of tiles (bought as blanks until 1881) and vases. Associated especially with revival of metallic oxide lustre colours and 'Persian' colours, particularly blues and greens. Wide inventive powers used for reproducing his attractively stylised, two-dimensional designs. Close friend of William Morris. In failing health, wrote successful novels.

Dentils Classical architectural feature used in 18th-century furniture cornice mouldings: series of regularly spaced small rectangular blocks protruding downward like row of teeth **(124)**.

46

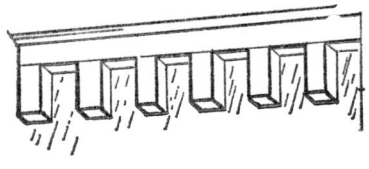

Derby From 1749 making soft-paste porcelain. 1755–86, Derby Porcelain Co. directed by *William Duesbury* (q.v.) making figures, ornaments **(125)**, useful wares **(368)**. Glassy frit paste with thick white glaze to 1770; thereafter bone ash in porcelain to *c.* 1805, close grained, with creamy translucency and enamel colours thinly applied. *Biscuit* (q.v.) figures *c.* 1773–1830. Marks included most familiar crown, crossed batons, dots and script D. Bone china from 1805, work deteriorating under ailing *Robert Bloor* (q.v) Factory closed 1848 but old Derby King-street premises reopened. From *c.* 1860 to 20th century old Derby mark revived with jewelled crown and script D but with crossed swords instead of batons and flanked by SH (for Stevenson & Hancock and, from 1866, for Sampson Hancock.) Derby Crown Porcelain Co. founded 1877; became Royal Crown Derby Porcelain Co. 1890.

123–124 Acanthus leaf design from Sheraton's *Drawing Book* (*left*) and dentil moulding in furniture cornice

125 Derby porcelain vase, late 18th century

126 Dessert glasses: for dry sweetmeats, custard, syllabub

Dessert glasses For 18th century's popular informal repast of sweetmeats, fruit, wines – forerunner of cocktail party. Included stemmed shallow glasses for dry sweets such as candied fruits **(126 left)** and wet sweetmeat glasses such as trumpet-bowled jellies, wide-mouthed double-ogee syllabub glasses **(126 right, 364)**, handled custard cups **(126 centre)**, thick conical ice-cream glasses. Also salvers to stand them on. See also *Pyramid*.

Diamond cutting Glass decanters and other vessels cut on revolving wheel in close patterns of diamond points, elaborated into 'hobnail' **(127 bottom)**, 'strawberry' **(127 top)** and so on. Imitations in pressed glass.

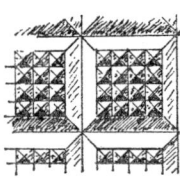

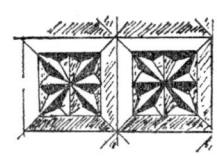

127 Diamond cutting – 'strawberry' (*top* and 'hobnail'

128 Dish cross, Sheffield plate

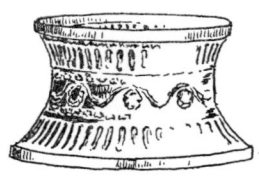

129 Dish ring, silver, chased and pierced

130 'Doctor Syntax landing at Calais'

Diamond point engraving on glass From 1720s, armorial; 1725–40, scroll patterns; early Victorian, coaching and other scenes. More engraving is wheel cut. See also *Engraved glass*.

Dish cross 1750s–1800s. Silver, Sheffield plate (**128**). X shape with pivoting arms radiating from central spirit-lamp: arms have adjustable brackets and feet to hold any size of round, oval or oblong serving dish over the flame which in a late model may have a disc to spread the heat. Open frame dish stand was simpler variant.

Dish ring Throughout 17th–18th centuries. Silver, brass, pewter, Sheffield plate. Hollow, somewhat waisted ring decoratively embossed, pierced, chased (**129**). Table-protecting stand for hot dish, or placed on dish to support napkin containing jacket-baked potatoes. Not exclusively Irish.

Dish wedges Silver, Sheffield plate, ceramics. Pair of triangles to tilt carving dish and facilitate spooning of juices.

Dished Table, tray or chair-seat surface lower than its rim (**523**).

Dished corner Slightly sunk area (circular, square) on table for candlestick or games counters.

Dr. Syntax ornament Thomas Rowlandson illustrations of fictitious character in William Combe's *Tours of Dr. Syntax*, (published in books, 1812, 1820, 1821), reproduced in aquatint prints (**130**: landing at Calais), on blue-and-white earthenware, and in mantelpiece figures (by Salt and others).

Dogs, ceramic Few in 18th–century porcelain, agate ware; 19th–century bone china. Mainly 1820s–50s, earthenware. Especially greyhounds, dalmatians, poodles and seated lapdogs (comforters). Many reproductions.

Dolls Adult figures called children's babies. Early, wooden heads (some wax); kid or linen bodies. Early 19th–century wax heads or moulded papier mâché. From 1850s some heads bone china; from 1855, parian ware; from 1862, strong biscuit porcelain. Wired for sleeping, walking, talking from 1820s. Light blue eyes mainly from *c.* 1840. See also *Pedlar dolls* and *Fortune dolls*.

Dolls' house Specimens remain from late 17th and early 18th centuries when known as baby-house; far more, in wide range of size and quality, from 19th century, splendidly equipped, especially from 1840s onwards. Also elaborate kitchens with English or German furnishings.

Door porter or door stop Mainly after 1775. Cast iron (**80**), some bronzed, and brass, cast in round with long handles. Flat backs from 1790s; some without handles from 1810. Celebrity figures from 1820s. Knight (**131**) registered 1841 and other Coalbrookdale figures now copied. Also in Derbyshire marble, Minton terracotta, glass. See also *Dump*.

Door rapper From 16th to end 19th century in wrought iron. From 18th century some heavy cast iron with wrought-iron rapper. From *c.* 1820 more styles and sizes wholly in malleable cast iron (**132**). From late 18th–century rapper more strongly attached. From early 19th century, brass. From 1839 some fine Coalbrookdale castings, sometimes marked.

Doulton wares From 1815, John Doulton (1793–1873) partner in stoneware pottery at Vauxhall, London: some celebrity figures, hunting jugs (**133 left**), mugs etc. (**413 left, 426**). Doulton & Watts at Lambeth from 1826. Son Henry born 1820. Mainly important domestic wares; art wares in collaboration with Lambeth School of Art (founded 1854) became important from 1860s, modellers including George Tinworth (terracotta) from 1866. Salt-glazed stoneware in unfired plastic state decorated with incised work, applied mould-shaped reliefs, stamping, raised slip work and high-temperature colour glazes. Richer colours from *c.* 1875 and wide range of treatment including etching, gesso, gilding. Most valuable pieces signed; work by assistants

131 Door porter: Coalbrookdale knight design

132 Door rapper or knocker

133 Doulton wares: hunting jug, 1820s (*left*) and art pottery, 1870s

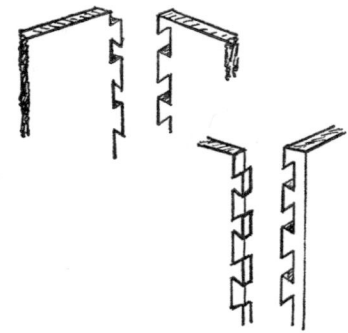

134 Dovetails, through (*top*) and lapped

135 Dram glass

136 Draw table, closed and open

usually X mark and number on base. 1882 also took over from Pinder, Bourne & Co., Burslem. 'Royal' from 1901. See also *Copper lustre, Lambeth faience, Majolica, Marqueterie ware, Silicon ware*.

Douter Silver, Sheffield plate, brass, iron. For extinguishing candle. Scissor action like snuffers but with flat discs for squeezing wick. Also cone shape for chamber candlestick (**53, 290, 500**), and with vertical handle from point of cone for use on candle protected by glass shade.

Dovetail From *c*. 1600. For joining end-grain wood as in drawer corners with fan-shaped projections fitting corresponding hollows. From *c*. 1700, under veneer, crude through dovetails (**134 top**) replaced by lapped dovetails (**134 bottom**) to avoid gluing veneer to end-grain.

Dowel pin From later 15th century. Headless wooden pin to secure *mortise-and-tenon joint* (q.v.), its slightly convex end often conspicuous detail of every joint in piece of early framed-up furniture – the original square peg in round hole, to ensure tight fit without glue (**287 top**).

Down hearth Most primitive form of fireplace with movable andirons to support burning wood on a flat slab of stone a few inches above floor level.

Dram glass From early 18th century. A Joey, a small sturdy vessel for spirits, with knop stem or brief stump above wide heavy foot (**135**). 1720–1850, might be trumpet bowl, short drawn stem. Nineteenth century included tumbler designs with ribbed bases.

Drawn stem 'Straw-shank'. Drinking-glass stem formed as drawn-out extension of bowl. Alternative is separately made bowl and stem (stuck-shank).

Draw table From late 16th century. With end flaps to draw out horizontally from under central section, supported by slanting bearers (**136**, closed and open).

Dresden On 19th-century English ceramics may be noted as pattern name. Never used on famous Dresden china made at Meissen, which used crossed swords marks, also popular on English would-be imitations.

Dresser From Tudor days, long side table for dining hall or parlour, where food might be assayed for poison. Rack of shelves attached above from *c.* 1700; row of drawers and pot-board or cupboards below. See also *Welsh dresser.*

Drop, glass From late 1730s. More from 1760s. Lustre. Pendant ornament for e.g. chandelier, girandole (**197**), epergne. Broad drop shape with faceted surface, followed by 19th century's long thin icicle, with vertical faceting. Sharp angular-cornered prisms from 1840 (**304**).

Dry edge figure Early soft porcelain characteristic, the glaze stopping short of the base so that its edge is rough and dry looking.

Drypoint engraving Variant of line engraving, with lines in copper plate hollowed out with a steel point, but leaving small burr or ridge of metal to the side of every stroke, giving resultant printed line a velvety edge. Also used by etchers to touch up acid-etched plate.

Dry stonewares See *Fine-stonewares.*

Duck egg porcelain 1816. Swansea porcelain showing clear greenish translucency against the light. Evolved by William Billingsley; made for only six months but reproduced.

Duesbury, William 1725?–86. Known first in London as independent ceramics decorator. With partners acquired Derby 1756, Chelsea 1769, Bow 1776. Followed by son (d. 1796) and grandson (to 1810).

Dumb waiter 18th–19th centuries. Variant of circular pillar and claw table with two (**137**) or three tiers in diminishing sizes on central pillar, for self-service at informal meals.

Dummy board figure Especially 17th–18th centuries. Flat board cut in silhouette and painted to resemble human (**138**) or animal figure, bowl of flowers and so on. Edges thinned from back ('softened') for greater realism. Used as house or garden ornament, often in empty fireplace.

Dump Victorian; cheap bottle-glass door stop, high-crowned, egg-shaped dome with long air bubbles trapped within the greenish glass (**139**).

Dust board From 17th century. Wooden partition between drawers in all cabinet-makers' chests of drawers.

137　Dumb waiter

138　Dummy board figure

139　Dump of greenish glass

51

140 Dutch oven, japanned iron

Dutch metal Brass alloy. Substitute for gold leaf. Used in powder form, as in papier mâché ornament.

Dutch oven Iron, copper, japanned metal (**140**). Shelved oven to be placed with its open back against grate.

Duty ace 1712–1863, payment of duty on playing-cards indicated by mark on ace of spades – amount of duty and monarch's initials. From 1765 part of duty indicated on the pack's wrapper. From 1862 whole duty (3*d*.) on wrapper but ace continued decorative. Forged duty aces are collected.

Dwight, J. See *Fulham stoneware*.

Early Georgian From 1714, accession of George I, to about 1760, accession of George II. Changes from Queen Anne style somewhat influenced by Hanoverian court. Introduction of mahogany such as carved chairs (**141**); porcelain following silver styles (**142**: Bow). Robust, vigorous style (**143**: pewter), heightened into rococo fantasy. See also *Georgian*.

Earthenware Wide general term for opaque ware, porous after kiln-firing so that it requires glazing before domestic use (**24, 102, 146, 204**).

Eastlake, C. L. 1836–1906. Influential *Hints on Household Taste* 1868. Practical middle-class interpretation of modified Gothic trends, away from meaningless curves to uncompromising structural straight lines and from florid carving to very low relief contrasts of texture and colour.

Ecuelle From 1700s in silver, saucer-shaped bowl with lid and pair of horizontal handles. Later 18th-century, in porcelain, some without handles.

Egg-and-dart, egg-and-tongue, echinus From 16th century on English furniture. Classical architectural ornament on mouldings and borders. Alternate oval and arrowhead shapes, carved in relief (**144 top**).

141–143 Three examples of early Georgian work: chair of 1730s, Bow porcelain of 1750s, pewter, early 18th century

144 Egg and dart furniture motif (*top*) and typical version of Greek key pattern

145 Egyptian motifs for furniture

146 Elevator, brown-glazed earthenware

147 Embossing on rococo silver jug

Egg frame From late 18th century. Silver, Sheffield plate. Stand holding egg cups and spoons (often gilded) around raised central feature which may be loop handle, toast rack or salt cellar.

Egyptian black stoneware From 1720s. Black fine-stoneware, impervious to liquids after a single high-temperature firing, needing no glaze. From 1770s improved by Wedgwood but still inferior to his twice-fired black *basaltes* (q.v.).

Egyptian ornament Mainly popular beginning of 19th century, following Napoleon's Egyptian expeditions. Carved Egyptian heads on pilasters (**145 left**); sphinx heads; lotus; scarabs; chimera-monopods (**145 right**); hieroglyphs.

Electro-plating Patented 1840 by Elkington & Co. of Birmingham, using electrolysis process (**85**). Wares made up in base metal and completely covered with thin film or frosting of silver from sheets of pure silver deposited by means of electric current (in contrast to Sheffield plate where the metals are fused together under heat before making up).

Electrotype Patent 1841. Electrolysis method associated with electro-plated silver applied to making exact reproductions of silver ornaments, classical antiques and other works of art.

Elers ware From *c.* 1690. J. P. and D. Elers, in England from Holland from 1688, used formula introduced by John Dwight (see *Fulham*) to make scrupulously refined, semi-vitrified fine-stoneware teapots resembling Chinese imports, thrown on wheel then trimmed on lathe, the ornament shaped with metal dies.

Elevators Nineteenth century. Earthenware, brightly coloured or in Rockingham glaze (**146**). Set of four blocks to raise a piece of plinth-based cabinet furniture about two inches above floor, such as a dresser standing on wet-mopped stone flags. Imaginative designs include celebrity heads, dogs, lions and lion paws, baskets of fruit as well as conventional bun shapes.

Elizabethan 1558–1603. Style much influenced by Italian Renaissance ornament, widely reproduced and adapted by early Victorians so that collectors view with caution all heavily carved oak furniture and elaborate iron mounts. Victorians also used term Elizabethan for distorted copies of 17th-century styles.

Embossing Silver (31, 147) and other metals. Relief ornament formed by pushing or punching from the underside. Silver thus embossed (repoussé work) is usually finished by flat chasing.

Empire style Now widely used in England for heavy classical style associated with Napoleon's first empire (1799–1815). Compares with English Regency period (1811–20). In both, style characteristics were associated with longer period – say 1795–1825. Confusing term English empire style wrongly implies English copying of French through period of almost ceaseless enmity.

Enamel glass From 1750s. White, opacified with tin oxide, much resembling porcelain. Decorated with enamel colours and transfer prints. Vases (148), candlesticks and so on, brittle and liable to surface scratching. From 1770s a cheaper *lime-soda-potash glass* (q.v.) was used.

Enamelled glass From *c.* 1720 in white; *c.* 1760–1820 in colours. Clear glass painted instead of being engraved, cut or etched. See also *Beilby, Cameo glass, Mary Gregory glass.*

Enamelling, ceramics From *c.* 1740s, colours composed of metallic oxides combined with lead oxide glaze painted on ware already glazed so that a further firing in kiln fuses them to the surface. Often each colour requires firing at a different temperature. Slow and costly process, improved from 1812.

Enamels, painted From 1740s. General term for products of Battersea (514) 1753–6, Birmingham and South Staffordshire's Bilston (40, 158) and Wednesbury (50, 502). Snuff-boxes, plaques, cutlery handles, candlesticks (149, showing top inverted for ornament). Fashioned in paper-thin copper, covered with fused-on opaque white enamel and decorated in enamels or transfer-printing. From *c.* 1760 raised gold scrolls, coloured backgrounds. Small cheap items from *c.* 1780s.

Enamel twist glass Mainly 1760–80. Spirals of coloured and opaque white glass within clear glass of wine glass stem (150).

Encaustic ornament Ancient 'burnt-in' method of fixing colours on ceramics with heated wax. Wedgwood, 1769, patented a range of encaustic colours – red, white, green,

148 Enamel glass, opaque white with painted flowers

149 Enamels, painted: covered vase, the lid inverted to make candlestick

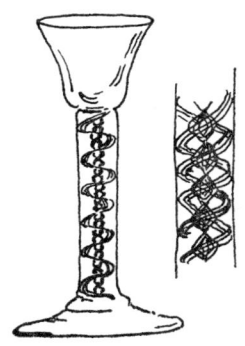

150 Enamel twists: two examples showing ribbons and threads of white and coloured enamels

black, bronze – for matt-surfaced ornament on, e.g. black basaltes, imitating classical designs.

End-of-day glass Victorian. Makers included Sowerby's Ellison Glassworks, Newcastle upon Tyne, who called it vitro-porcelain. Now also known as slag glass because it incorporated steelworks slag drawn off at end of day. Press-shaped spill vases (**151**), baskets, butter dishes and so on, usually in white-streaked marbled purples, blues or browns. May show diamond shaped *registration-of-design mark* (q.v.), in use 1842–83.

151 End-of-day glass: press-shaped spill vase

Engine turning 18th–19th centuries on silver; fine stonewares from *c*. 1760 (**152, 231, 345**). Delicate symmetrical patterns mechanically engraved as unostentatious impersonal ornament by use of lathe with eccentric motion. Began as wood turner's device, used, e.g., for shaping piecrust tables.

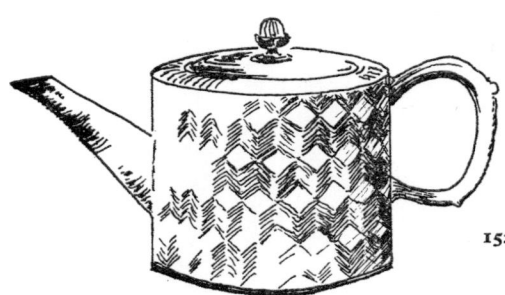

152 Engine turning pattern in low relief on late 18th-century stoneware teapot

ENGLAND ceramics mark From 1891, not earlier. McKinley Tariff Act required the name on wares exported to U.S. so that many firms found it convenient to include it in their trade mark. MADE IN ENGLAND is 20th-century variant.

Engraved glass From 1730s. Ornament cut by holding glass vessel against revolving wheel (**3, 179, 370**). Narrow borders at first; polished from *c*. 1740. See also *Diamond cutting* and *Diamond point engraving*.

Engraved print, line engraving From 15th century. Impression from metal plate incised with cutting tool (burin), the displaced metal being removed and the tapering hollows filled with printing ink. Damped paper pressed heavily upon the clean-wiped plate extracts the ink. Much used 18th–19th centuries for commercial reproductive work. See also *Wood engraving*.

Engraved silver Linear ornament cut – not hammered – into surface with range of sharp, pointed tools, removing tiny fragments of the metal **(76)**. See also *Bright cutting*.

Entrée dish Silver, Sheffield plate, ceramics. Mainly from 1740s. For presenting made-up foods (cook's specialities) as distinct from joint. Often kept warm on matching hot water vessel **(153)**. Close-fitting lid. Circular, soon followed by square, oblong, rectangle with incurved corners. Shallow lids followed by higher domes *c.* 1800. Often a flat lid, with removable handle, could serve as second dish.

153 Entrée dish lifted off its stand (warmed with hot water)

EPBM mark From 1840s. Wares superficially resembling silver constructed in the hard pewter known as *Britannia metal* and finished by *electro-plating* (qq.v.).

Epergne From *c.* 1760. Glass, silver, Sheffield plate. Centrepiece for dining-table with curved branches supporting detachable dishes for fruit, sweetmeats, pickles **(154)**. May have sauce and condiment vessels below.

EPNS mark From 1840s. More familiar than above. Ware silver-covered by electroplating over a base of nickel alloy.

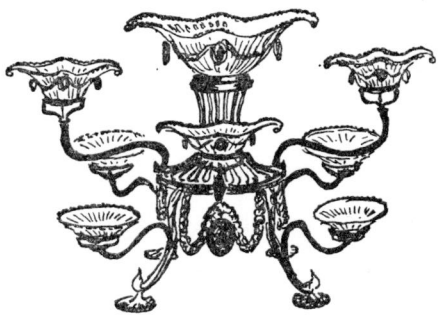

154 Epergne, silver, 1774

Escallop shell Silver, Sheffield plate, mould-shaped white stoneware, porcelain, furniture ornament. Badge adopted by medieval pilgrims to shrine of St James at Compostella. Silver: embossed shape for 17th-century jugs, sugar or spice boxes **(155 bottom)**; 18th–19th–century baskets, table dishes, with blue glass linings from *c.* 1760. Furniture especially early 18th–century carving such as cabriole leg knees **(155 top)**; later, frequent marquetry motif.

155 Escallop shells: cabriole chair leg carving (*top*) and on silver spice box

Escutcheon (1) Silver, glass and so on. Shield shape for coat-of-arms or other personal device **(65)**. (2) Iron, brass, ivory, mother-of-pearl. Plate in decorative outline pierced for keyhole, often with pivoting cover **(156)**.

Etched glass Patent 1857 by Benjamin Richardson, on *cased glass* (q.v.) (earlier on plain glass.) Ornament cut through outer layers of colour by applying hydrofluoric acid to lines scratched through acid-resistant wax covering. This could be speeded from 1890s by applying acid around design printed in acid-resistant ink. Shallower and less desirable than hand cutting.

156 Escutcheon on 1750s furniture

57

157 Etruscan style (1851 exhibit by T. Battam)

Etching, print Lines cut with needle tool through protective wax varnish to expose copper plate which is then 'bitten' by aquafortis, forming hollows. As with line engraving, the print is taken under great pressure from the ink-filled hollows. Such lines appear freer than line-engraved work, less clear-cut and with blunt instead of tapering ends.

Etruria 1769–1940; then Barlaston. Ceramics factory founded by *Josiah Wedgwood* with partner, Thomas Bentley, following renewal of interest in Etruscan pottery due to excavations.

Etruscan style From *c.* 1760s, part of neo-classic mood attempting to imitate excavated ancient Etruscan vases with much use of contrasting *encaustic* colour (q.v.). Important Victorian vogue, especially from 1840s (**157**: by T. Battam, 1851).

Etui Especially 18th century. Gold and gold-harnessed hard-stones, painted enamel, pinchbeck, porcelain, ivory and so on. In 17th century known also as tweezer-case or tweezer. Lady's small case, to carry or hang on châtelaine, partitioned for scissors, tweezers, snuff spoon, ivory memo slips and similar personal details. Most often flattened, slightly tapering cylinder, the upper third a hinged lid (**158 right, 328, 502**). Cube-shaped box (**158 left**) similarly fitted, now usually called by French name of *nécessaire* but probably names originally interchangeable.

158 Etui, painted enamel (*right*) and style now known as a *nécessaire*

Eye portraits Ornament on ivory and tortoiseshell snuff-boxes and in jewellery. Painted by late 18th–century miniaturists, delicate at first, coarser later. By 1830s stock designs painted in enamels obtainable from jewellers for mounting as required. Victorian vogue for life-size specimens framed in pearls and attached to mantelpiece.

Facet cutting From *c.* 1720s. Glass. Shallow hollows ground into surface, making patterns of diamonds, triangles and so on **(159 left)**. Very shallow pre-1740; more elaborate from 1770s; less important than heavy diamond cutting from 1800s.

160 Faïence (Lambeth) vase

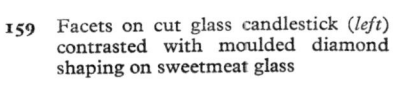

159 Facets on cut glass candlestick (*left*) contrasted with moulded diamond shaping on sweetmeat glass

Facsimile Exact copy or reproduction, e.g. of an engraving, as distinct from an original print. Not usually of collector interest.

Faïence Alternative term for maiolica or delftware (earthenware covered with opaque white tin-enamel) but now sometimes applied to earthenware covered with white engobe or pipeclay. See also *Tin-enamelled earthenware* and *Lambeth faïence* **(160)**.

Fall front From late 17th century. Fitted writing cabinet or bureau drawer with front opening down to provide writing area **(161)**.

Fan From 1580s folding style gradually out-moded plumes. Endlessly changing size and

161 Fall front desk

162–163 Two fans: late 18th-century cabriolet (*top*) and Victorian with gilded mother-of-pearl sticks

164 Feather posy, Victorian

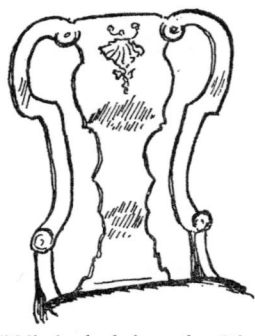

165 Fiddle-back chair, early 18th century

extent of spread **(162)**. Many remain from Victorian vogue for earlier styles.

Fan blades or sticks Ivory, gilt-enriched mother of pearl, **(163)**, tortoiseshell, horn, sandalwood. Early, the brin or visible part of stick was long and narrow, each with complete pattern carved, pierced, painted. During 18th century became broader, overlapping, with unified pattern extending across them. *Brisé fan* (q.v.) was composed of ribbon-linked sticks without mount.

Fan guards End sticks, stronger and broader than rest to protect brins and mount when fan was closed. Handsomely ornamented with jewels, gilding, carved pearl.

Fan mounts, leaves From late 16th century in supple vellum cut in lacy patterns and edged with gold or silver lace. From later 17th-century vellum (see *Chicken skin*) painted in pliant gouache. In 18th–19th centuries also silks, lace, paper. Printed outlines, hand coloured, may aid dating.

Feather work Through 18th century, amateur hobby. Bird ornaments, flower sprays and so on composed of feathers cleaned, trimmed and attached by gum arabic one by one to paper-covered panel. Popular again from 1830s when feathers might be bleached white and spray-dyed although some makers boasted they used no dye or tint **(164:** Victorian feather posy).

Fecit Latin: **he made**, usually with a name. Under a print indicates etcher or engraver as distinct from painter of original picture (*pinxit*).

Feldspar porcelain Mainly *c.* 1800–1830s. Evolved by Josiah Spode II. Harder, more translucent than bone china. High quality table wares. Made also by Chamberlain of Worcester, Derby, Coalport and others.

Fender From late 17th century, to edge hearth; sheet iron for common use. From 1700s some steel pierced and engraved. From late 18th century some, more substantial, of brass with iron bottom plate. From mid-1820s also cast iron.

Fiddle-back chair From 1700s. Chair in body-fitting, bended-back style, with either side rails or central splat in waisted outline suggesting violin **(165)**.

Fiddle-back table silver From 1800s. Spoon or fork, with rounded-rectangular end and square shoulder (**166 left**: with variants shell-and-thread, king's, Albert, Victoria).

Fiddle-back veneer Wood with fine streaky rippled grain suggesting the maple wood used for backs of high-quality violins.

Field bed 16th–19th century term; also slope bed. Traveller's bed quickly assembled and space-saving. Curtains essential for warmth and privacy hung on light frame, arched or slanting.

Fielded panel Typical of 18th–century panelling. Flat-surfaced panel with sunken bevelled edges, the field projecting slightly more than its framing.

Filigree, metal Gold or silver wire formed into delicately curled and twisted ornament (**167**). Imitated in 19th–century press-stamped gilt-metal work such as posy holders (**337**).

Filigree paper work Early ecclesiastical use. From *c.* 1650s with seed pearls and other enrichment as amateur hobby. Some fine knife-cut vellum. Popular later 18th century, for decorating boxes (**168**), screens, framed panels. Narrow strips of stiffened paper variously rolled and curled and attached to wooden surface by gluing edge-on. With projecting edge coloured or gilded they suggested metal filigree.

Filter, stoneware Through 19th century important for water purification. Handsome five-gallon cylindrical vessel with handles, lift-off cover and base tap. Often surface-ornamented in low relief, sometimes including maker's name (**169**: Doulton). Improved design by Henry Doulton, 1870.

Fine-stonewares 18th–century improvements on *stonewares* (q.v.) similarly rendered watertight by great heat instead of needing glaze. Included: *red stoneware*, sometimes called *Elers ware*; *Egyptian black* and Wedgwood's improvement known as black *basaltes*; *cane-ware*, *c.* 1770; *jasper ware*, 1774 (qq.v.). Also known as dry stonewares.

Finial Ornament at top as on cabinet cornice, teapot lid, spoon handle. Typified by late 18th-century urns (**198, 452**).

Finger bowl From *c.* 1760. Glass bowl, plain rimmed, often confused with *wine glass*

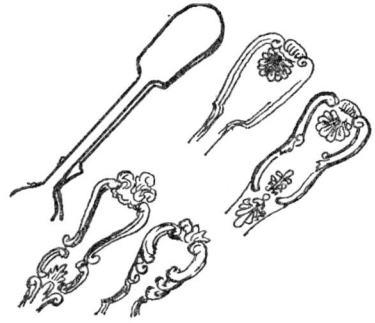

166   Fiddle spoon and variants (shell-and-thread, king's, Albert, Victoria)

167   Filigree work in silver

168   Filigree paper ornament

169   Filter in Doulton stoneware

170 Firebacks

171 Fireclay conservatory vase, Victorian

172 Fishley candlestick and cream jug

cooler (q.v.) which has one or two rim indentations for wine-glass stems.

Fireback   From later 15th century. Slab of cast iron set vertically at back of fire to throw out heat and protect chimney wall. Early wide rectangle followed by early 17th–century rounded top and late 17th–century scroll-topped tombstone shape (**170**). Ornament included in casting may aid dating.

Fireclay ware   Victorian. Conservatory ornaments, wine coolers and other massive black stoneware vessels (**171**) in cheaper substitute for basaltes. Ornament in relief or white enamel.

Fire polishing   Glass. Re-heating glassware at furnace to remove manufacturing blemishes such as marks of mould or press so that clean surface and smooth edges suggest hand-cut glass.

Firing glass   From 1760s. Stumpy dram glass (**135**) on thick short stem with heavy disc foot for rapping on table as form of acclamation.

Fishley earthenware   Fremington, Devon. Name sometimes found on early-looking 'peasant' wares in yellow-glazed red earthenware (**172**) and white earthenware hand-painted in red, some with 18th–century dates. These were mainly late Victorian products when pottery was owned by first Fishley's grandson, Edwin Fishley.

Fish trowel   From 1750s. Silver, Sheffield plate (**173**). With triangular blade with intricate saw-cut pattern for serving whitebait. From 1770s, narrower fish slice; less elaborate piercing augmented by engraving. Fish-shaped blade 1780s–1820s; some diamond-shaped from 1780s; an asymmetrical design with one bevelled edge introduced c. 1800. Fish serving-fork from 1820s.

Fitzroy barometer   Victorian. Patent registered 1881, 20 years after death of inventor, Admiral Fitzroy. First inexpensive barometer in cheap rectangular case with fully visible mercury tube sometimes with thermometer and storm glass, also practical weather-lore (**174**).

173   Fish servers, *c.* 1750s, 1780s, 1800s

Flagon Silver, mainly ecclesiastical. Pewter, from 17th century as serving vessel. Tall, slightly conical and spoutless with hinged lid raised by thumb-piece over D-shaped handle. Beaked lip from *c.* 1720. Regency Oxford flagon had urn-shaped body and double-dome lid (**175**: early 18th century including scrolling 'Yorkshire' shape).

Flame stitch embroidery Florentine stitch. From later 17th century. Popular for furniture. Vertical stitch worked on counted threads of canvas, entirely covering it in series of zigzags or conventional flames, the colours carefully aligned and somewhat suggesting the marbling on paper and pottery. Florentine untwisted silk often replaced by worsted crewels in English work.

Flashed glass Victorian. Cheap variant of cased glass, gathering of glass being inflated then dipped briefly into molten coloured glass which formed thin film on surface. Could apply several layers of colour before reheating and shaping.

Flask See *Spirit flask.*

Flatback ornament Victorian. Ceramic figure or group usually shaped in a single mould which necessitated somewhat pyramidal design. Relief detail and colour restricted to front and sides, for mantelshelf display. Many topical subjects – royalty, political celebrities, poets, representative Crimean war figures (**176**: 'Miss Nightingale') and so on. Many reproductions.

Flat chasing See *Chasing.*

Flatware General term for plates, dishes, as distinct from hollow-ware vessels.

Flemish scroll S-shape composed of sharply opposing curves, frequent as arm support or front leg of William III chair (**177**).

Flint-glass From 1674 (e.g. **3, 42, 79, 107, 197, 198, 223**). Silica essential for glass-making introduced in form of powdered calcined flint. Lead oxide added 1675. Important English development by George Ravenscroft. Heavier, with far richer refractive power than Continental soda glass. Resonant ring when struck. Improved especially *c.* 1740 and 1780. Now often called lead crystal.

174 Fitzroy barometer

175 Flagons, early 18th century

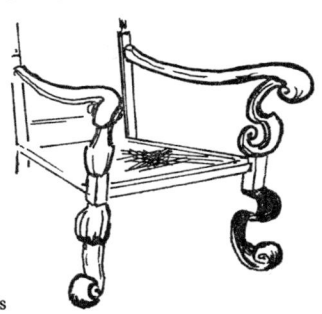

176 Flat-back figure group – 'Miss Nightingale'

177 Flemish scrolls

63

Flowered glass 1740s–80s. Flower-engraved, small-capacity drinking glass **(107)** for the potent cordials sipped with evening tea and thus harmonising with porcelain teacups.

Flower-encrusted china From 1750s, porcelain, some white biscuit; far more from *c.* 1820s, bone china; a little, coarse, earthenware; from 1850s, a little parian ware. Carnations, roses, zinnias, and so on, modelled in round, naturally-coloured and attached to vessels, candlesticks and ornaments **(99, 178)**, including cottage-shaped pastille burners **(109)**.

178 Flower encrustations on bone china ornaments

179 Flute glass for cyder

Flown blue From *c.* 1820. Evolved by Wedgwood firm and widely used by Victorian potters, the blue ornament spreading slightly into surrounding glass with soft halo effect. Occasionally other colours from 1830s.

Flute From 1680s. Drinking glass with deep conical bowl to contain sediment expected in strong ale, cider and other drinks. From 1740s often engraved with appropriate hop-and-barley or fruiting apple tree **(179)**. Champagne served in flutes until 1715 and 1730s–1830s. Long flutes, 10–14 ins., only in soda glass until *c.* 1800.

Fluting Furniture, silver. Especially late 18th century. Classical ornament composed of series of parallel concave channels in contrast to convex reedings. In furniture applied to pilasters **(324)**, table legs, usually introduced vertically. In silver **(284, 306)** often on thin factory-made vessels strengthened slightly against denting by the surface corrugations. See also *Bat's-wing fluting* and *Petal fluting*.

Fly bracket Furniture. Rail, hinged at one end to swing out horizontally and support flap of pembroke or other light table.

Food warmer See *Veilleuse*.

Footman Iron and brass four-footed variant of trivet to stand before fire grate (180).

Fore-edge painting Medieval use for book titles in libraries; from *c.* 1520 (Thomas Berthelet) for ornament, painted in specially prepared water colours over ground colour. Painted on edges of book pages tightly clamped, to be seen only when book is closed; popular variant from mid-17th century was 'disappearing picture' visible only when pages were slanted or fanned (181). Double painting from 1790s meant pages showed ornament whichever way they were slanted. Painting often concealed by gilding while book tightly closed; rarely by marbling. Much amateur work around 1800. Popular early 19th century, especially landscapes, and still in production, age of book being no guide to age of painting.

Forks From 17th century in considerable use. Silver, with two, three or four tines – number no indication of age but four most usual from 1750s. For dating, steel forks, including those with silver handles, can be compared with style of accompanying knives; early silver forks with harmonising spoons. Silver dessert knives and forks widely used from early 18th century.

Fortune doll Mainly Victorian. Customary petticoats replaced by folded paper slips printed or inscribed with non-committal prophecies (e.g. *For love and war you'll travel far*) to be pulled open at random; books of replacements were available.

Four-poster bed From late 17th century, standing bed, that is with tester and hanging curtains. In 18th century indicated bed with low head-board that needed tall posts at all corners (182).

Foxing Rusty-looking marks found on old prints, often where damp has affected traces of iron in hand-made paper.

Free-blown glass High-quality vessel shaped by glass blower without using moulds.

French foot Furniture. Especially late 18th century, chests of drawers (183), cabinet furniture. Bracket foot which curves smoothly outward in dipping line instead of being vertical or S-shaped on outer edge.

French polish Much used on furniture from 1820s. Shellac dissolved in methylated spirits suitably dyed and applied repeatedly to protect veneer from damp. New furniture

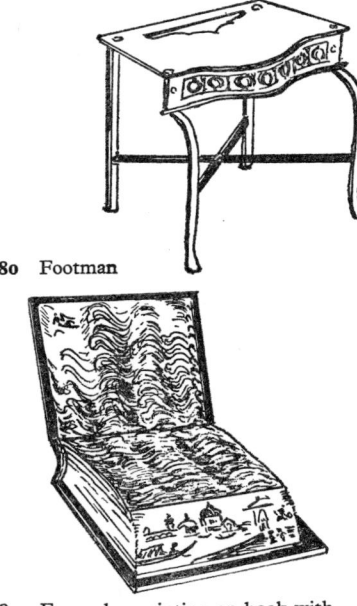

180 Footman

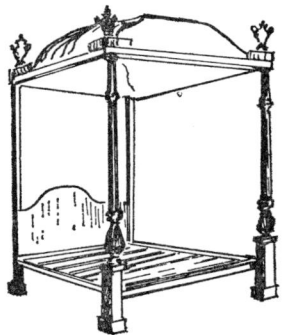

181 Fore-edge painting on book with marbled end-papers

182 Four-poster, 18th century

183 French feet on chest of drawers

E 65

184 'Frigger' of spun glass

185 Frog mug

186 Frye's Bow porcelain, *c.* 1760

treated in course of construction. Also applied to earlier furniture. Glossy, hard, but affected by heat and lacking glow of normally-polished wood.

Frigger Glass. 18th and especially 19th centuries. Collectors' term for imitative 'toy' such as top hat or hunting horn, approved for its novelty and implied skill but with no known association with apprentice work. Elaborate groups – ships, birds-and-fountains (**184**) – rivalled porcelain ornament but much was cheap fancy work by street-corner virtuoso manipulating heated rods of glass to 'spin' animals, shoes, walking-sticks. Reproductions common.

Frit Mixture of sand and alkalis used to make glass and, mixed with clays, to make glassy translucent ceramic (soft-paste or frit porcelain) when potters lacked ingredients for true porcelain.

Frog mug Late 18th to mid–19th centuries. Earthenware. Joke drinking mug with full relief model of frog or toad, sometimes two, 'climbing up' inside towards drinker's mouth (**185**). Widely made. Dated by general shape, colouring, weight of mug. Mainly now found in heavy Victorian granite ware.

Frosting Silver. Popular early Victorian treatment with acid fumes to obtain matt white surface on parts of elaborate ornament which might have other detail highly polished and partly gilded. Glass ornaments silvered by patent of 1848 might be partially frosted by grinding.

Frye, Thomas 1710–62. Irish mezzotint engraver remembered today for important soft-paste porcelain manufactory, Bow (**142, 186**), where he was works manager and patentee of formulae and processes.

Fulham stoneware Factory founded 1671 by John Dwight who obtained patent for making stoneware and evolved or developed brown, white, a mottled 'agate' and an unglazed red. Dwight died 1703 but pottery continued by his family. *John Doulton* (q.v.) was apprentice at Fulham.

Fumed oak From end of 19th century. Furniture surface greyed with ammonia fumes, fading to yellowish tone. Not to be confused with early 20th–century limed oak with lime preparation showing whitish where brushed into grain.

Gadroon ornament knurling, nulling. 16th century onwards. To edge furniture, silver (**187**) and other metals. Series of convex knobs or knuckles often separated by narrow flutes; upright or slanting.

Galena glaze   See *Lead glaze.*

Games table   Mainly from 1750s, including pillar and sofa tables (**188**). Very popular early 19th century. Fitted with reversible flap marked on one side for chess and draughts and often covering shallow well for form of back-gammon known as tric-trac. Often with drawers for pieces and sometimes small rectangular tablets for cribbage scores.

Gallery   Especially late 18th century onwards. Raised border to table or tray, usually consisting of tiny spindles or pierced metal fret (**51, 120**).

Garnish   Pewter. Set of dozen each of platters, plates and bowls.

Gate-leg table   From 17th century and still being made. Hanging flaps to sides of central fixed top are raised to rest on additional legs hinged into table under-framing and leg stretchers (**189**). Flap was listed as falling leaf, as distinct from folding leaf.

187   Gadroons on silver candlestick

188   Games table (drawers are sham)

189   Gate-leg table

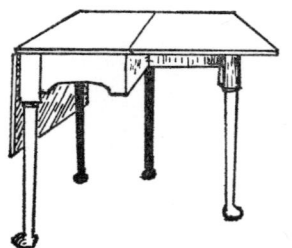

190 Gate table

191 Gesso ornament covering side table

192 Gilding on furniture (Chippendale bracket design)

193 Gilding on glass to suggest silver-gilt label

Gate table Introduced in early Georgian mahogany, the wood being so strong that no stretchers were needed to link the legs. This meant that table required only four legs even with both flaps extended, as two could be swung out, on vertical hinges, with parts of the under-framing (**190**).

Gather Glass. Blob of hot molten glass that the glass-blower gathers on end of blow-pipe to expand into hollow globe.

Georgian period Variously interpreted. Most usually divided into early Georgian (George I and II 1714–27 and 1727–60); George III (1760–1820) including Regency (1811–20); late Georgian (George IV, 1820–30, who was followed by William IV before Victoria came to throne in 1837).

German silver 19th-century alloy of copper, zinc and nickel containing no silver. Used as substitute for silver (table ware and so on), advertised from 1835 as argentan plate. Also from c. 1820 used as core to which silver was fused under heat, taking place of copper in Sheffield plate and preferred because inconspicuous when silver surface wore thin.

Gesso Especially early 18th century. Expensive ornament on tables (**191**), stools. Paste prepared from whiting and parchment size: applied to flat or carved pinewood to build up low-relief pattern delicately tooled and water gilded.

Gibbons, Grinling 1648–1720. Fine designer and sculptor in stone as well as superb wood carver of delicate wreaths, pendant swags, cherubs. But great amount ascribed to him is merely of his school or style. Out of fashion by 1720 but much imitated by early Victorians.

Gilding on ceramics From early 18th-century impermanent oil gilding; from 1755 dullish honey gilding; from c. 1785 brassy mercury gilding. Early 19th century, solid gilding, e.g. on Spode bone china from 1810 (**219**); occasional underglaze gilding; rare transfer gilding (improved 1835). Brilliant, impermanent liquid gold on cheap wares from c. 1855; rich burnished brown-gold from 1860s. Acid gilding (etched patterns in low relief) invented 1862 by J. L. Hughes for Mintons.

Gilding on furniture Popular in England from 1660s and for much ornament through the 18th century (**192**: Chippendale bracket).

Filmy gold leaf attached by suitable mordant to prepared wood surface: gesso composition essential under costly water gilding. Oil gilding cheaper than water gilding and more damp-resistant, but could not be burnished or double-gilded.

Gilding on glass (Often little remains.) Rims often gilded 1715–90; bowls 1760–90. Bright mercury gilding from 1780s; sparkling liquid gold from *c.* 1855. (**193**: 'label' on blue glass decanter.)

Gilding on metal Ancient process of fire gilding applied to furniture mounts (**194**) of brassy alloys such as bronze – the mid-Georgian's ormolu introduced by *Matthew Boulton*. Powdered gold applied in mercury amalgam which was dispersed by heat, producing dangerous fumes. Electro-gilding like electro-plating in silver from 1840s.

Gilding on papier mâché Especially popular from 1820s. Gold variously tinted with alloys from 1840s.

Gillow firm, Lancaster Important furniture makers. London showrooms from 1770. Furniture stamped with their name occasionally from 1790s and generally after 1820.

Gilt metals Brassy alloys gilded as above to prevent tarnish. Substitutes for gold, increasingly used through 18th–19th centuries for inexpensive 'toys' such as châtelaines, buttons, counters, mounts of English enamel bijouterie. Cheaper than *rolled gold* (q.v.) Some fine quality brass given golden appearance by dipping, but not tarnish-free unless in constant use. See also *Brass* and *Pinchbeck*.

Gimmel flask Two bottles surface-fused together to form single unit internally divided and separately spouted for, e.g. oil and vinegar. Popular in cheap flecked glass now known as *Nailsea* (**195**).

Gimson, Ernest 1864–1918. Furniture designer (**196**) inspired by Morris with apprentice-experience of traditional country chair-making.

Girandole From late 17th century but mainly from about mid-18th. Glass, gilded metal, gilded composition on wire core. Term variously applied to *candelabrum* (q.v.) and wall *sconce*, supporting two or more candles. Associated with extravagant rococo design and subsequent neo-classic elegance. Name used especially for cascade effects achieved with

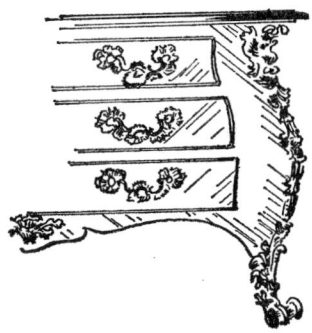

194 Gilding on mid-Georgian metal furniture mounts

195 Gimmel flask ('Nailsea' glass)

196 Gimson-designed cabinet on stand

197 Girandole candlestick

198 Goblet and cover (glass with gilded rim)

199 Gothic windsor chair, 18th century

swags and pendants of glass lustres or drops, popular from 1780s. Simple variant then was pair of girandole-candlesticks **(197)** with shoulder-circles of lustres.

Glass print (1) From late 17th century, especially late 18th century, deteriorating in early 19th. Mezzotint print affixed with clear varnish face down upon clear glass and the soft paper damped and rubbed away, leaving print outlines on back of glass, to be hand painted from behind. (2) 19th century. Sheet of opacified glass drawn upon by artist so that his lines let sunlight fall upon light-sensitive paper.

Glaze, ceramic Basically, essential surface covering to render porous earthenware or porcelain watertight. Simplest was galena (see *Lead glaze*). Some stained with metallic oxides, yellow, green, manganese purple and so on. Ware could be dipped in liquid glaze from 1750. See also *Lustre, Salt glaze, Smear glaze*.

Glazing bars Furniture. Wooden strips linking panes of glass on cabinet **(58)** and the like. Narrower and decoratively arranged supporting thinner glass from 1750s.

Goblet Glass drinking vessel on stem and foot with broad, deep bowl, blown-moulded or pressed, offering great scope for ornament – wheel engraving **(370)**, crystal cameo, gilding, casing. Some with tall finialed covers **(198)**. Also found in ceramics such as 19th-century lustreware.

Gold leaf Almost pure gold repeatedly hammered into filmy-thin sheets fixed by 'breathing' on to prepared size. See also *Gilding*.

Gold lustre Ceramic ornament important in early 19th century, covering or patterning surface with extremely thin film of hard lustrous metal fixed by firing. Tone ranged from bright gold to copper and mauve by use of gold oxide with alloys. At first applied over glaze. After 1823 often over reddish brown clay; sometimes over wash of gold-tin alloy (purple of cassius) to achieve shot-silk sparkle.

Goss, W. H. Stoke-upon-Trent. From 1858 made fine quality parian ware including ornaments, busts, biscuit porcelain jewellery and hand-modelled flowers; terracotta. From 1892 renowned for miniature articles in ivory-tinted porcelain bearing brilliantly coloured coats of arms.

70

'Gothic' furniture Especially around 1750s (**199**: chair back) and through 19th century. Minor enthusiasm for romantic-medieval 'church-window' ornament as escape from neo-classic graces, on normal basic structure, and often mingled with 'Chinese' whimsy.

Gothic taste Concerned with design as well as ornament. Based on medieval (12th–14th century) as distinct from classical ideals. From early 18th century with baroque associations in architecture including sham castles, ruins, to early 19th-century phase as part of romantic's quest for the picturesque. Serious approach initiated by A. W. N. Pugin (1812–52) and Sir George Gilbert Scott. Late Victorian Gothic included more popular 'middle-class' simplicity of, e.g. *Bruce Talbert* and *Charles Eastlake* (qq.v.) (Simple Victorian applications: **171**; **200**: jug by Meigh, glass and silver vase.)

Graham, George 1673–1751. Clocks and astronomical instruments. Inventions included dead-beat escapement (1715) and mercury pendulum.

Grainger, Thomas Worcester porcelain decorator who, with partners, had bone china factory from 1812 (**201**). Later made lithophanes, parian ware. Taken over by Royal Worcester Porcelain Co. in 1902.

Graining 16th century onwards. Colour and figure of oak, walnut and other valuable woods imitated by painting and combing cheaper woods and, in 19th century, cast iron.

Grandfather clock 19th-century name for *long-case clock* (q.v.) made in England from 1660s.

Grate Some 17th century but mainly from 18th, when wrought iron or steel basket grate; also, from 1750s by cast-iron hob grate (**202**) with smaller opening flanked by flat-topped solid panels ornamented in relief. Raised fire, controlled draught (some had register valve) and held it compactly for burning coal.

Greek leg Early 19th century, often as disproportionately heavy front leg to dining-chair. Wide below small flattened ball knee then tapering quickly to small ankle swellings: often with heavy reeded or fluted ornament (**203**).

Green glass Flint-glass vessels in fashion through most of 18th and 19th centuries. Cheaper bottle glass, pale green from 1800s (**139**), for ornaments and curios decorated with murky colours and trails of white (now called *Nailsea*).

200 Gothic-Victorian jug by Meigh, 1842 (*left*) and glass and silver vase

201 Grainger bone china basket dish

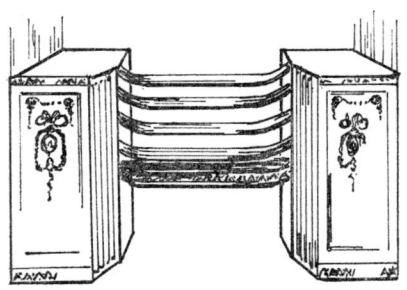

202 Hob grate, early 18th century

203 Greek leg

204 Green glaze ware, Wedgwood

Green glaze ware From 1750s and made ever since. Developed by Josiah Wedgwood mainly for table ware, including many leaf shapes. Underlying earthenware dark toned until 1775, then lighter (**204**). From late 1790s translucent deep green of copper oxide supplemented, but not wholly replaced, by more opaque chromium oxide green in wide range of tints.

Grisaille From late 18th century. Ancient painted wall ornament adapted to porcelain, furniture panels, fans, glass, more or less subtly imitating original notion of creating three-dimensional effects by cumulative layers of semi-translucent greyish-white tone. Notable on 1850s Worcester porcelain.

Gros-point embroidery See *Cross-stitch*.

Grotesques Furniture, silver, all periods including considerable use in late Victorian marquetry. Ornament painted, carved or engraved with intertwining foliage and scrolls (arabesques) fantastically mingled with human and animal detail. (**205**: by J. Tijou, 1693).

Guilloche Furniture. Greek architectural motif. From 16th century in English carving. Intertwining circles in a plaited ribbon effect with considerable variation of detail (**206**).

Guipure d'art Popular Victorian hobby. Geometrical patterns in coarse thread darned in range of stitches with blunt needle on squares of machine-made net. For large covers, squares joined by tatting or crochet.

205 Grotesques in ironwork design by J. Tijou, 1693

206 Guilloche motif

Hair mementoes Especially around 1800 and early Victorian. Shaped by specialist 'craftsmen in human hair' into flower knots, plumes for lockets and the like. Hair embroidery popular for watch-backs. Delicate print-like pictorial embroidery, 1780s–1840s **(207)**, but often scene worked mainly in black silk, such as springy unravelled piece-silk. Horsehair ornaments especially from early 19th century: plaited and interwoven as cheap costume 'jewellery' such as bracelets, rings, muff chains – light, resilient, suggesting delicacy of filigree, in natural colours or dyed.

Hall chair From 1730s, but many 19th century. Essentially single (no arms) chair with plain wooden seat and back to serve waiting messenger and sedan chairman in rough outdoor clothes. Back often painted with impressive crest or cypher and seat slightly dished to make well-polished surface less slippery **(208)**. Chippendale included summer-house use.

Hallmark From *c.* 1300. On gold and silver plate, small punch mark indicating hall or office where its quality had been assayed or tested. Accompanying marks indicate year of testing, maker and quality – all now loosely termed hallmarks **(63)**. London hallmark is so-called leopard's head **(209**: before and after 1820). See also *Carat, Date letter, Lion marks on silver.*

Hand raising Silver. Traditional craftsman's way of shaping flat silver plate into bowl shape, by prolonged hammering interspersed by annealing with heat to make it tough, not springy. Finished to even, lustrous surface by form of hammering called planishing.

Hard-paste porcelain English-made from 1768. Porcelain according to Oriental formula containing china-stone and china-clay, both obtained from felspar rock at different stages of decay and fired at very high temperature, *c.* 1450° F. Harder, colder brilliance than imi-

207 Hair memorial embroidery, *c.* 1800

208 Hall chair, Regency

209 Hallmarks, silver: 'leopard's head' before and after 1820

210 Harpsichord, 1760s

211 Hen, parian ware, by J. & M. P. Bell

212 Hepplewhite design, looking glass

213 Herculaneum china mark

tative soft-paste porcelain and with ringing tone when struck. Made at Plymouth (**48**), Bristol and New Hall (**298**) but much now found in England was imported from Continent – Meissen (made from 1708), Sèvres (hard paste from 1769) and many other factories.

Hard wood Any wood from broad-leaved tree (angiosperm) – oak, beech, walnut, mahogany – regardless of physical hardness, as distinct from pine, fir and other gymnosperms.

Harewood Late 18th–century use of English sycamore and maple wood stained greenish grey with oxide of iron, then known as silver wood. Used in marquetry. John Evelyn in 17th century referred to aier wood.

Harpsichord From 16th century. Elaborated version of spinet. Stringed instrument in shape of recumbent harp with one or more keyboards, the strings plucked by quills when keys are depressed (**210**: *c.* 1760s).

Hens, ceramic Through 18th–19th centuries. Crudely modelled ornament on top of cheap pottery moneybox (nest-egg idea). Sitting on nest, associated with other porcelain bird tureens for serving desserts. In bone china, as 'gift wrapping' 1820s–30s; later for serving breakfast eggs; also in mid-Victorian parian ware (**211**: by J. & M. P. Bell). In coarse pottery from 1840s, as sweet-filled fairings.

Hepplewhite, George 1788, first edition of his furniture designs – *The Cabinet Maker and Upholsterer's Guide* – published two years after his death. Preface claimed that it reflected the latest styles of period, a pleasantly simple, flowing adaptation of Adam neo-classicism (**212, 317**). No furniture made by him is known.

Herculaneum Liverpool. Late 1790s–1841, ceramics. Excavations of classic Roman art prompted English use of such famous names (cf. Wedgwood's factory village, Etruria). Well-decorated, marked, earthenware and bone china in Staffordshire styles. Mark of liver bird with sprig of liverwort (**213**).

Herringbone banding Especially early 18th century, on furniture. Lines to suggest rectangular panels introduced into flat veneers. Composed of two very narrow lines of veneer side by side with opposing diagonal grains. Mitred corners on good English work (**214**).

High temperature colours Ceramic colours that can endure heat of glazing kiln so that they have protection of glaze. Essential for, e.g. tin enamelled ware and popular because wearing well on everyday vessels with relief-moulded patterns where overglaze colours would soon flake. See *Pratt ware*. Include blue (from cobalt), yellow (antimony), purple (manganese), brownish orange (iron rust), red (iron oxide) and mixtures to obtain intermediate tones such as green and turquoise. By mid-19th century nickel brown, chromium green and red, platinum grey, iridium black and red tones from oxide of gold were added.

Hob grate See *Grate*.

Hollow stem *c.* 1760–75 and 1830s–40s. Drinking glass with bowl and stem drawn in single piece so that wine sediment remained in stem when glass was tilted. Cut ornament made it inconspicuous. Early Victorian use was in wide-bowled champagne glasses but cleaning proved difficult.

Honeypot Especially around 1750s and 1850s. Silver (**215**), ceramics, pressed glass. Identifiable when made in shape of plaited bee skip with lid and stand as during recurrent vogues for table wares in naturalistic forms.

Honeysuckle ornament See *Anthemion*.

Hope, Thomas 1769–1830. Connoisseur, encouraging interest in revival of Grecian and Egyptian styles. His *Household Furniture and Interior Decoration*, 1807, illustrated furniture, in extreme classical, architectural taste, of his Deepdene, Surrey, home (**256, 262**).

Horn Of cattle, rams, buffalo, flattened and split into plates, also carved, turned and – softened by heat – shaped in moulds. Cheap, non-burning, pliant, for lantern windows, table wares, knife hafts (called scales). Somewhat grained surface but cheap substitute (stained) for tortoiseshell in combs, snuffboxes (**216**: snuff mull), brisé fans often with applied ornament in metal, ivory. Many 19th-century beakers, spill vases; some modern with engraved ornament.

Horse brasses Mostly from 1850s on (**217**). Small ornamental discs with shoulder loops hung from harness of cart and dray horses. Colour and quality of brass is guide to dating. Cast motif soldered to loop or crescent was largely replaced by flat stamped design from 1870s. Portraits mainly late souvenirs. 'Antiqued', carelessly-finished, modern castings abound.

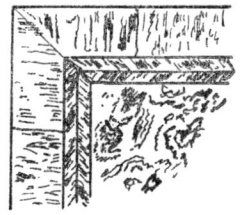

214 Herringbone banding in walnut veneer

215 Honeypot, silver

216 Ram's horn snuff mull

217 Horse brass

75

218 Huguenot style: tea kettle by Paul de Lamerie and two of his marks

Horse furniture See *Cheval furniture*.

Hour-glass See *Sand-glass*.

Huguenot work 1685 Revocation of Edict of Nantes prompted many persecuted French Protestants to bring their crafts to England where in Spitalfields, London, silk weaving was already established. Influence reflected in much ornate early 18th-century silver with foliated strapwork, complex handles, profile heads. *Paul de Lamerie* (q.v.) (**218**: typical work and marks on sterling and Britannia standard silver), Pierre Harache and Augustin Courtauld were of Huguenot descent.

Ice pail Silver, china. Lidded vase or bucket for iced water with inner straight-sided lining for single bottle of wine at dinner-table (**219**). Proportions determined by changing shape and size of bottles (becoming taller, narrower.)

Image toys 18th-century term for primitive ceramic figures. (**220**: tortoiseshell and agate wares).

Impressed marks Ceramics. Stamped into clay before firing or glazing: more laborious to fake on old wares than painted marks. Alternative is more variable incised mark cut freehand into the ware.

Ince, William and Mayhew, John Cabinet makers remembered for designs in their *Universal System of Household Furniture* which appeared in parts 1759–63, showing elaborate rococo and Gothic ornament (**221, 261**).

Incised ornament Ceramics. Especially slipware when pictorial work and inscriptions are cut through outer layer of slip to appear in underlying contrasting body colour. Sometimes called sgraffito work to distinguish it from sgraffiato work where background is cut away.

Incised twist 1740–1800. Drinking glass. Straight stem cut with incisions while plastic and immediately twisted (**179**). More closely corrugated from 1760s.

'India' or 'Right India' 17th–18th-century term for Oriental lacquer, porcelain and so on, imported by East India Co.

219 Ice pail (Spode) showing four parts

220 Image toys, tortoise shell and agate wares

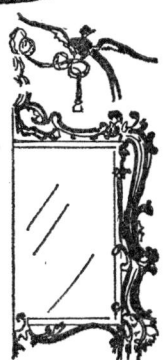

221 Ince & Mayhew picture frame design

222 Inlay, 17th century

223 Irish glass, late 18th century

224 Ironstone china ewer and basin

Inlay Mainly from 17th century when known as set work (**222**). Furniture pattern made by inserting small pieces of contrasting woods, ivory, metal, shell, in hollows cut in solid wood, in contrast to marquetry which was worked wholly in veneers.

Intaglio Implies that design is cut into surface in contrast to relievo work where background is cut away. Hence motif cut into seal matrix, and copper plate engraved or etched for making prints.

'Irish Chippendale' Especially around 1760s. Modern term: no direct connection with Chippendale and not necessarily Irish. Ornate versions of contemporaneous furniture styles including such detail as massive carved table aprons, hocked cabriole legs.

Irish glass Mainly from late 18th century. Export permitted from 1784 and escaped heavy English glass tax until 1825: hence some massive pieces (**498**) such as fruit bowls (**223**), butter dishes, decanters. A few *lozenge* and *vesica* patterns (q.v.) may be claimed as Irish, but in general indistinguishable from English except for occasional marked piece. See also *Blue tint* and *Waterford glass*.

Ironstone china Patented 1813 by C. J. Mason. Slightly translucent earthenware, hard, white, with clear ringing tone (**224**: ewer and basin). Bright colours in confused flower patterns on table wares, conservatory vases, garden seats. Continued from 1861 by Ashworth & Brothers, sometimes with Mason marks.

Italian Comedy figures From 1750s copied in English soft-paste porcelain from Meissen hard porcelain; also in 19th-century bone china. Colourful Harlequin, Columbine, Pierrot, Pantaloon and others from Italian *Commedia dell' Arte*.

'Italian' quilting Popular from 18th century for light bed covers using double layer of fabric usually without interlining. Pattern outlined in double lines of stitches through both layers and the tunnel so formed filled with soft cord or candlewick (**225**).

225 'Italian' quilting detail

Ivory Elephant's modified tooth substance, its transverse section showing tiny curving lines forming minute lozenge-shaped spaces – inconspicuous in good quality (**226**: showing contrasting textures of ivory and bone; **76**). African close-textured, glossy; Indian more densely white and easier to work. Also from other animals and Victorian 'vegetable ivory'. Obvious substitute was brittle, splintering *bone* (q.v.).

Ivory porcelain From 1856. Worcester development of parian ware. Biscuit figures; costly paper-thin hollow ware; ornaments sometimes decorated with film of silver or bronze.

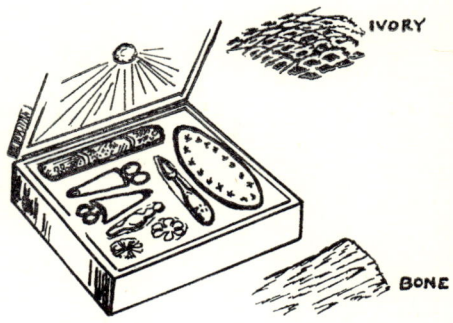

226 Ivory compendium fittings: details show textures of ivory (*top*) and bone

79

227 Jackfield ware teapot

228 Jacobite drinking glass

229 Japan pattern, porcelain (Worcester kylin detail)

Jackfield, Shropshire From 1751. Now generic term for jet-black wares – dark earthenware dipped in deep blue glaze and fired in smoky smother-kiln. Often gilded ornament. Popular late 18th–19th centuries **(227)**.

Jacobean Made in reign of James I (1603–25). Also sometimes the term late-Jacobean applied to fast-changing styles of James II's reign (1685–88). General term for 17th century. Victorians adapted many Jacobean features for what they called Elizabethan style.

Jacobite glass Mainly 1740s and later. Drinking glasses associated with clubs fostering propaganda for Old and Young Pretenders, especially the 1745 rebellion. Engraved with more or less cryptic. rose, star, butterfly, such words as *Fiat* and *Revirescit* and crude portraits **(228**: jay bird and Jacob's ladder plant). Very often spurious engraving on old glasses.

Japan patterns, ceramic From mid–18th century on Chelsea, Bow, delicate, at first in Kakiemon style **(186, 350)**, then rich 'brocaded' wares. Distinctive Worcester work in full range of styles **(229**: Oriental kylin pattern). Popular on early 19th-century bone china as artless arrangements of exotic flowers, especially in velvety blue, iron red, lavish gold, which deteriorated from c. 1830. In 1870s new wave of 'Japanesque' design and ornament. See *Brocaded Imari*.

Japanning, metal Good quality from c. 1730s. See *Pontypool, Usk*. Some at Bilston from 1702, Wolverhampton from 1720, Birmingham (Baskerville) from 1750.

Japanning, wood From 1660s. Furniture, imitating Oriental lacquer but using heat-hardened spirit varnishes (later sometimes cheaper oil varnishes). Pseudo-Oriental motifs on glossy, richly coloured grounds **(230)**, some with low relief (gesso) ornament covered in dullish raised gilding. Especially on early 18th-century long-case clocks but spasmodically on minor furniture through 18th and 19th centuries. Reproductions: see *Crazing*.

230 Japanning on wood (typical gilded detail)

231 Jasper ware: engine-turned dice pattern, Wedgwood

Jasper dip From 1785. White jasper ware (see below) dipped in a coloured jasper solution. Less valuable than solid jasper ware. Widely imitated.

Jasper ware From 1774 to present day. Wedgwood's extremely hard fine-stoneware containing barium sulphate, vitrified so that its fine-grained surface needed no glaze. Vases, table wares (**231**), cameos, plaques. Solid jasper was coloured throughout its body – soft blue, sage and olive green, black, lilac, yellow.

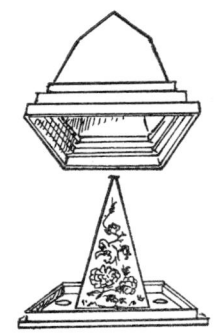

232 Jelly mould, two parts

Jelly glass Early 18th century, waisted trumpet bowl, straight stem, pair of double-loop handles. About 1725–50, no handles, knop joining bowl and foot. From 1740s, bell-shaped bowl, soon directly on domed foot (**159**). Shallow ornament, followed from 1790s by deep cutting and square foot.

Jelly mould From 1730s, white salt-glazed stoneware, very small, fluted. From 1770s larger, in Wedgwood creamware consisting of fluted mould and central cone or pyramid. Cone, flower-ornamented, put upside-down inside mould and hot jelly poured in. When mould was lifted off, the cone remained to prop the jelly (**232**). From 1840s heavy stoneware moulds, much cheaper than period's moulds in Britannia metal and tinned copper.

Jennens & Bettridge, Birmingham 1816–64. Successors to *Henry Clay* (q.v.) Largest makers of high quality papier mâché, known as paper ware, which may be found impressed

233 Jet, carved paper knife

F

234 Jewelled porcelain, Worcester

235 Joggled work on pewter tankard

236 Joint stool, early 17th century

with their name from 1820. 'Makers to the Queen' included in mark from 1840 (**310**, **311**).

Jet Black form of lignite. English form especially hard and takes brilliant polish (**233**: paper knife). Popular for Victorian bijouterie but widely copied in cold black glass, also in vulcanite and in moulded blackened wood powder.

Jet ware See *Jackfield.*

Jewelled porcelain From 1850, introduced by W. T. Copeland (from Sèvres, 1770). Coloured enamel dotted on to circles of gold foil, fixed by firing to porcelain glaze. More permanent method by Goss from 1872. Such ornament also by Minton, Worcester (**234**), E. Wedgwood & Co.

Joggled work Simple ornament by itinerant workers on early soft pewter, more distinctive than alternatives of light engraving, punched chasing or pricking. Flat tool held at angle and pushed with rocking motion to make series of small curved cuts (**235**: 17th-century tankard).

Joined furniture From about 15th century. Strongly, neatly constructed by fitting framework together (end grain tenoned into side grain) with mortise and tenon joints secured with wooden dowel pins. In fashionable work gradually augmented by cabinet maker's techniques from 1660s.

Joint stool Typical of joined furniture. Sturdy stool with seat framing and stretchers tenoned into the legs which were left in square section for these joints (**236**). In contrast to turner-made stool with free-standing legs driven into holes in the block seat (Windsor chair style, **373**).

Kaendler, J. J. 1706–75. Important as originator of the porcelain figure style copied by all early English makers, such as Chelsea, Bow, Derby. Chief modeller at Meissen (Dresden) 1731–75.

Kauffmann, Angelica 1741–1807. Swiss-born artist working in London 1766–82. Employed by Adam for painted ceilings and murals. Adaptations of her work, such as her picture of Sterne's *Maria* widely used by commercial decorators for painted medallions on furniture (not her own handiwork). Her name, spelt Kauffman, noted on some late 19th-century German porcelain.

Kent, William 1686–1748. Probably earliest English architect specialising in interior decoration, in massive but disciplined *Palladian* manner (q.v.), one of small but influential group reviving style of long-misunderstood Inigo Jones. Important from 1720s as painter, decorator, designer of lavish furniture in massive scrolled and pedimented manner (**237**) and landscape gardens.

Kerr & Binns, Worcester 1852–62. Important period for Worcester Porcelain Company with great technical advances and over 600 workmen (**238**: marks). Introduced familiar mark of four cursive Ws in circle, the mark being topped by a crown from 1862.

Kick Mainly pre-1760. Glass. Hollow in base of bottle or decanter, appearing as rounded hummock inside vessel. Assisted early method of *annealing* (q.v.).

King's blue Mainly *c.* 1820–40. Admired by George IV. Glass of rich purplish-blue coloured with refined Saxony cobalt (smalt), named to distinguish it from cheaper synthetic blues.

Kiln wasters. Found around scene of past potteries. Fragments of ceramic wares dis-

237 Kent style table detail

238 Kerr & Binns china marks (with partly concealed date)

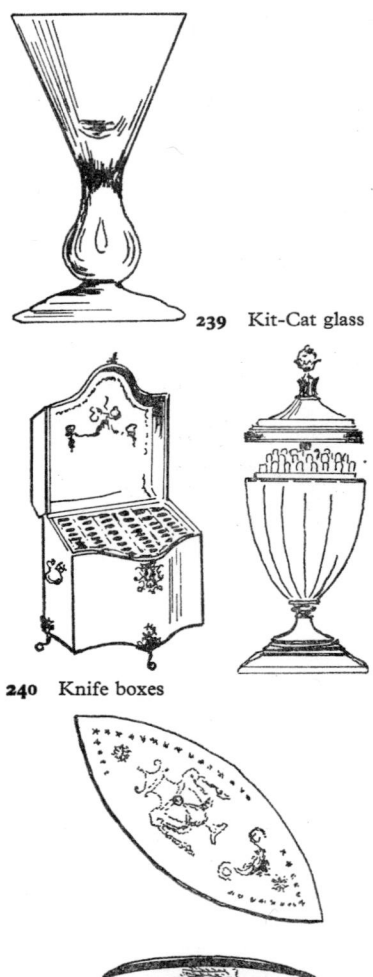

239 Kit-Cat glass

240 Knife boxes

241 Knotting shuttle (two views) with piqué ornament

242 Knurled foot, two views

carded for flaws in course of manufacture and always worth careful scrutiny.

Kit-Cat glass Early 18th century. Drinking glass with heavy-based funnel bowl and baluster stem on folded foot, the design illustrated by Kneller when he painted members of the Kit-Cat Club (**239**).

Knife box From 17th century. Small chest with slanting lid partitioned to hold table knives, forks, spoons on end, ensuring that any theft would be conspicuous. Specialist craft producing exquisite work by later 18th century when a pair of boxes would stand on sideboard pedestals. By then many were in urn or vase shape with lid rising on central stem (**240**).

Knop Swelling introduced as ornament in drinking glass stem (**3, 198, 457**) as distinct from baluster curve. Many self-explanatory names – acorn, mushroom, button, angular, ball and smaller bullet and slightly flattened cushion. Often several together (multiple). May be hollow but more often solid, perhaps with central air bubble 'tear'.

Knotting By 1690 recognised as 'candlelight work' to ease the eyes. Popularised by Mary II. Early 'string of beads' style elaborated during 18th century for fringes and for couched ornament on fabric. Knotting shuttle then large and often costly: George III gave gold one to Mrs. Delany in 1783 at period when shuttle shape of pointed-end ellipse dominated ornamental design. Shuttles of cut steel, metal filigree, ivory, tortoisehell (**241**), bone. See also *Macramé* and *Tatting*.

Knurled foot Around 1750s. Furniture. Contemporaneous with scroll foot but in downward, curved-under outline, vaguely suggesting knuckles (**242**).

Kronheim & Co Victorian colour printers. From 1849 were among licensees of the *Baxter* (q.v.) process. Small prints in pocketbooks, Christmas cards may be charming, with delicate line engraving and stipple, together with clean, transparent colours.

Laburnum wood From 1660s. Important for decorative furniture. Veneer slicer cut across sapling or branch applied as 'oyster shell' parquetry showing irregular concentric growth rings, in brown, greenish and yellow tones (308).

Lace From 16th century. (1) Braid of gold, silver-gilt or silver for trimming men's clothing. (2) Cord for clothing and purses, its making a popular 17th-century pastime. (3) Delicate patterned mesh created in thread. See also *Needlepoint, Bobbin, Bone* and *Pillow lace.*

Lace box Especially later 17th-18th centuries. Now popular name for flattish rectangular box ornamented with marquetry (243), parquetry or embroidery, suitable for storing cuffs, gloves and other dress accessories.

Lace work, ceramic 19th century. Perforated lacy porcelain for dresses on figures – for example, in Minton parian ware. Technique originated in Rouen: machine-made lace soaked in wet ceramic slip, dried and oven fired, which consumed the cotton, leaving pattern in porcelain.

Lacquer (1) Ancient Oriental process using gum of tree *rhus vernicifera*. Popular from 17th century in imports into England of panels, cabinets, screens with hard glossy surface and brilliant colouring. Variously imitated in England by professionals and amateurs on wood and metal with stove-hardened varnishes known as *japanning* (q.v.). (2) Transparent solution of shellac dissolved in alcohol for protecting brass from tarnish. From 17th century sometimes tinted to golden tone.

Ladles Mainly silver, Sheffield plate, Britannia metal, electro-plate; some ceramic. Spoon with cup-shaped bowl, especially for dry tea-leaves, the hot drink punch (244) and self-served creams and sauces at formal meals.

243 Lace box with marquetry ornament

(See also *Caddy ladle* and *Punch ladle*.) On smaller scale, familiar with salts and mustard pots and once common in table snuff-boxes.

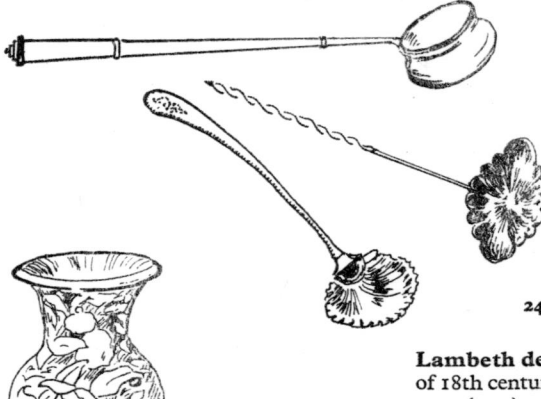

244   Ladles, *c.* 1700's, 1730's, 1750's

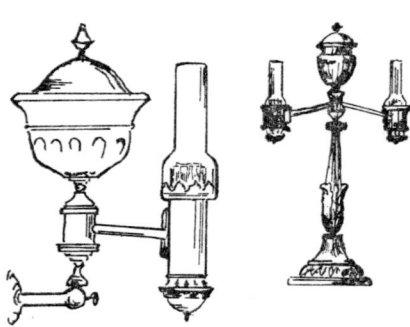

245   Lambeth faïence vase

Lambeth delft From *c.* 1660s through most of 18th century. Usual name for all *tin enamelled ware* (q.v.) made in Thames-side London.

Lambeth 'faïence' From 1873. Made by *Doulton* (q.v.). Fine earthenware fired to biscuit form then painted – flowers, figures, landscapes – before glazing and refiring **(160, 245)**. Sometimes surface modelling and gilding. Until 1900 warm yellowish lead glaze; thereafter leadless glaze. Artists and technicians studied 16th–17th-century maiolica and produced vases, cups, pilgrim bottles, plaques, tiles. More costly, finely coloured 'Crown Lambeth' from 1892.

Lamerie, P. de Huguenot silversmith at work in London 1711–51. Great influence on English design and workmanship in light, decorative rococo manner applied to candelabra, epergnes and so on **(218)**.

Lamps Through 18th century mainly for cottage, workshop, bedroom, burning only cheap smelly oils **(305)**. But brass and Wedgwood jasper ware in neo-classic design (hanging and pedestal) from 1770s with improved ribbon wicks **(246)**. See *Open-flame lamps*.

Lancashire chair Now popular name for: (1) 18th-century Netherlands design with rush seat and tall ladder back, the rails in shaped outlines; (2) 19th-century massive windsor with heavy, ornamentally turned spindles as arm supports, legs and stretchers.

Lancashire snuff-box 19th century. Strongly made brass or copper. Traditional watchmaking skill prompted Prescot makers to introduce ingenious combination locks worked by pointers on crudely engraved dials **(247)**.

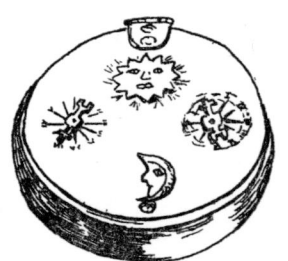

246   Lamps, *c.* 1810 (*left*) and Argand

247   Lancashire snuff-box

86

Included sun and moon ornament and inscribed memorial specimens.

Lantern Common from Middle Ages to modern times. Usually iron or brass with candle flame frequently protected by thin sheets of horn. From 18th century fashionable in costly multi-candle designs as ceiling or wall fitments for halls, staircases, with glass windows framed in gilded metal or carved walnut or mahogany (**248**: Chippendale design).

Lantern clock From late 16th century, the earliest English domestic clock (**249**). Metal frame with corner pillars and rounded bell dome; also known as birdcage clock. Worked by hanging weights, so slung on wall. Continued to early 19th century, but from late 17th century many wooden-cased, as long-case (grandfather) clocks.

Latten Common medieval term, eventually applied only to the kind of brass (yellow alloy of copper and calamine) that had been hammered into tough, close-textured sheets (**494**). Some English from 1580s; some machine-rolled from 1730s; heavy sheets flattened by steam-driven machines from early 19th century.

Lead glass From 1675. Vastly important English development by George Ravenscroft. He introduced *flint-glass* (q.v.) 1764, then greatly improved it by adding lead oxide. Double flint-glass contained twice as much lead as 'single', being durable, weighty, with great refractive power and resonant tone.

Lead glaze Earliest was galena or natural sulphide of lead sprinkled as powder on ware before kiln-firing when it acquired a more or less yellow tone. From 1750 alternative was clear liquid lead glaze (lead oxide). Leadless glaze, less noxious to workmen, used at Coalport from 1820. See also *Glaze, ceramic*.

Leather Animal skins and hides made flexible and durable by boiling or tanning. Used to cover early chests, chairs, some painted or gilded. Morocco (goat skin) popular from around 1750. Wall hangings from late 17th century might be embossed by blocking and tooling and sized, gilded and varnished. Much that remains dates to 19th century (Vessels such as black jack **41** and bottle **250**).

Le Blond print Full colour print in style made popular by George Baxter (see *Baxter prints*). Abraham Le Blond (b. 1819) bought some of Baxter's equipment in 1868, reissuing

248 Lantern, Chippendale design

249 Lantern clock

250 Leather bottle

251 Leeds glass-stand and teapot, late 18th century

252 Ley metal wine measure

253 Lignum vitae mortar

the prints less meticulously finished (now called Le Blond-Baxters). Also issued 125 different original prints – ovals – with mounts and labels and much other minor work.

Leeds ware 1760–1878. Leading makers of cream-coloured earthenware, very light in weight, with glassy glaze and often undecorated. Table ware, including ornate centre pieces, cruets, pickle stands (353). Typical detail includes delicate hand-punch piercing and double-intertwined handles (251). All association with original Leeds Pottery lost in 1820.

Lehr, glass maker's Oven for toughening – annealing – glass-ware by heating and slow cooling. From 1740s glass might pass through 18-foot tunnel lehr for some hours from hot to cold. Thicker glass annealed in improved lehr from 1780s. Lehrs made compulsory by 1810 Excise Act.

Leopard's head mark See *Hallmarks, Lion marks on silver*.

Ley metal Cheapest form of *pewter* (q.v.), heavily leaded, for candle moulds, wine measures (252) and so on. 'Thundercloud' tone might indicate up to 40 per cent of poisonous lead, reduced to a permitted maximum of 10 per cent in 1907.

Lignum vitae One of few foreign (tropical) woods imported before 1650 and long valued medicinally. Contrasting brown and black tones, occasionally used in veneer. Exceptional density and decay-resistance suited to lathe-turned machine parts and such large, deep vessels as wassail bowls and mortars (253).

Limed oak See *Fumed oak*.

Lime-soda glass Usual Continental glass. Quick cooling, thin, fragile, much imported until 17th-century development of English lead-flint glass. *Lime glass*, again with soda and lime as flux, introduced by William Leighton, West Virginia, 1864, as cheap but fragile glass for moulded and pressed work.

Lime-soda-potash glass From 1770s. Term for milky white glass opacified with arsenic or bone ash, evolved as cheaper alternative to white *enamel glass* (q.v.). Fiery opalescence seen against light. Hence popular name of sunset glow. Blown-moulded jugs, ornaments.

Limited, Ltd., on ceramics From 1860.

Included in mark accompanying a manufacturer's name. Indicates manufacture after limited liability was defined by law.

Linenfold ornament Especially 16th century, on panelled furniture. Probably Flemish origin. Panels carved in slight corrugations suggesting drapery, to prevent warping (254). Much used in recent reproductions.

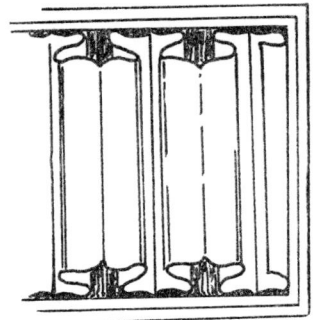

254 Linenfold carved panel

Lion marks on silver Found among row of hallmarks. Dating aided by changes in style and in puncheon outlines (255). *Lion passant gardant* (walking to left with head turned full face) mark of sterling silver (top left); looking ahead (*lion passant*) on London silver from 1820 but no change on some provincial work (bottom right). *Lion's head erased* (head side view, cut off at neck with wavy line) one of marks on *Britannia* (q.v.) or high standard silver (63). *Leopard's head* (heraldic lion's head full-face), crowned until 1820, used from 14th century on sterling silver hallmarked by London assay office and used occasionally by provincial towns (209). *Lion rampant* (255 top right) Scottish mark from 1819 (often crowned on Dutch silver). Minor lion details found in some marks of Chester, York, Norwich (255 bottom left).

255 Lion marks on silver

Lion ornament Furniture. Carved lion mask, leg and paw (256: T. Hope design) recurrently popular in early and late Georgian periods but with distinctive change to more formal shape and treatment; brass through Regency (Lion paws 17, 359).

Lithograph Invented 1790s. Surface print taken from prepared limestone, zinc or aluminium by drawing on it in greasy lithographic crayon or ink, or on prepared paper for transfer to the stone. See also *Chromolithograph* and *Surface print*.

Lithophane In England from 1828, patent rights held by Grainger, Lee & Co., Worcester. Other firms after 1842. Intaglio moulding in thin glassy porcelain. Against a light the humps and hollows form a picture. Mounted in window panels, lampshades, hand firescreens and so on.

Liverpool earthenwares From late 17th century; tin-enamelled ware from 1700s displaced by cream-coloured ware from 1780s. See also *Herculaneum*.

Liverpool porcelain Soft paste, greyish, rarely marked (257). Soapstone porcelain made from 1756 by Richard Chaffers, slightly

256 Lion ornament (Thomas Hope design, 1807)

257 Liverpool porcelain teapot

258 Livery cupboard, 17th century

259 Long-case clocks: late 17th century; early and later 18th century

260 Longton Hall porcelain, pickle plate and mug

261 Looking-glass frame, Ince & Mayhew design, c. 1760

grey body, faintly bluish glaze. Followed by P. Christian, 1765–early 1770s. From 1780s, Seth Pennington; Zachariah Barnes. Bone china made from 1800 by Herculaneum factory.

Livery cupboard From 16th century. Open 'board' for setting out food and candles carried by household to their rooms for night. Development of cupboarding shown in two-shelf variant, including small cupboard with chamfered sides (258).

Loggerhead Circular inkwell on broad, flat base, its rim containing holes for pens.

Long-case clock From 1660s. Familiar as grandfather clock, its weights and pendulum housed in wooden frame to stand on floor (259: late 17th, early and later 18th centuries). From 1690s maker's name on dial. Slender at first, with small dial (c. 10 ins. diameter), plain case. Larger, arched dial from 1720s. White enamel dial popular through later 18th century when case tended to be broad and ornate. But many throughout 18th century were plain with brass dials, easily ante-dated.

Longton Hall Short-lived, elusive soft-paste porcelain factory of the 1750s managed by Staffordshire potter, William Littler (260).

Looking-glass Small while depending on early process of blowing glass into cylinder and splitting open while hot; larger when cast in shallow trays as invented by Perrot, 1688, but very costly. Cast glass finished by glass grinders, smoothing both surfaces for undistorted reflection. 'Silvered' with tin and mercury amalgam under foil – silver, in fact, only from early Victorian days (261: early example of convex design by *Ince and Mayhew*, q.v.).

Loo table Now popular name for any 19th-century centre table in period's common design with circular top on central pillar and spreading pedestal or feet. Sometimes scalloped or eight-sided top from 1850s. Could be used for 18th–19th century card game in which loser paid a loo or forfeit.

Loper From the late 17th century, runner or slip. Rectangular-sectioned rail drawn out from slot or groove to support fall-flap of desk (161, 230).

Lotus ornament 'Water lily of the Nile', popular as flower or bud on Egyptian-style furniture of Regency (262: design by *T. Hope*, q.v.).

Loudon, John About 1783–1843. Important for such works as his vast *Encyclopaedia of Cottage, Farm and Villa Architecture and Furniture*, 1833, influencing home design and much factory-made furniture through Victoria's reign.

Louis XV style French king (1715–74) but in England style associated with light-hearted asymmetrical ornament of the rococo expressed in much furniture, silver, bijouterie, around mid-18th century and again extravagantly popular with early Victorians.

Louis XVI style French king (1774–93). In England expressed in somewhat severe elegance of much neo-classic design in Hepplewhite and Sheraton styles of 1780s–1800s; again popular in Victorian reproductions.

262 Lotus motif (Hope, 1807)

Love-spoon, Welsh Through 18th century recognised betrothal token carved by giver from single piece of wood. Ornamental handle from *c.* 1750s, becoming expansive pierced panel. From *c.* 1820 could be bought at fairs and more freely given; some machine-carved 1845–80, some with 17th–18th century dates. Identifiable carved motifs include Menai Bridge, opened 1826 (**263 right**), cage design containing balls, from early 19th century (**263 left**), and turnbuckle and chain (from seaman's rigging device patented 1870s). Double spoon bowls from *c.* 1850.

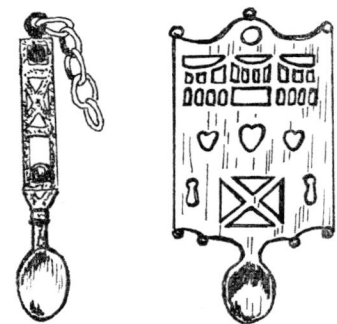
263 Love-spoons – turnbuckle and cage (*left*) and Menai Bridge outline

Loving cup From late 17th century as stemmed, two-handled grace cup; subsequently as toasting cup. Silver, pewter, slipware, white stoneware (**299**), glass. 1770s–1870s mainly lead-glazed earthenwares of Staffordshire, Leeds, often painted with name and date for owner (**264**).

264 Loving cup dated 1838

Lowestoft porcelain 1757–*c.* 1800. Softpaste porcelain strengthened with bone ash, easily stained but seldom crazed. Small factory meeting local needs for tea-ware, sauce boats and the like, individually initialled and dated mugs, birth plaques and so on and, in later years, souvenir 'Trifle from Lowestoft' pieces (**265**). Ornament relief-moulded, blue-painted underglaze and, from 1770s, sometimes transfer-printed or in enamel colours. Some copying of Worcester. But entirely different from so-called Chinese or Oriental Lowestoft which is hard-paste porcelain made in China for European market.

265 Lowestoft souvenir teapot

Lozenge ornament Diamond shapes, especially typical of 17th-century chest panel ornament, carved or incised.

Lustres, ceramic From *c.* 1790s. Metallic oxide suspended in solution brushed on to earthenware or bone china and fired in muffle oven to appear as extremely thin iridescent film of metal, sometimes leaving reserves for painted or transfer-printed ornament. See also *Copper, Silver, Sunderland lustres, Mother of pearl ware.*

Lustres, glass Mainly from late 1750s in especially brilliant flint-glass. Pendant drops facet-cut to achieve maximum light dispersal. Rounded drop followed from 1790s by elongated icicle shape. Sharp angular shaping for greater brilliance, introduced 1840. See also *Girandole*. Name given also to Victorian glass mantelpiece ornaments, vase shape, hung with long drops **(304)**.

Lyre ornament Shape constructed or carved in wood with metal 'strings' used as back of Adam style chair of *c.* 1770s **(266)** and in end support of Regency sofa table, with some Victorian repercussions.

266 Lyre motif in Adam style chair

Macramé work Popular Victorian hobby, successor to knotting for fringes (267) and so on but worked entirely with fingers and pins on lace-maker's pillow, twisting and plaiting a number of cords, silk twists or gold and silver threads.

Madeley, Shropshire 1825–40, unmarked soft-paste porcelain manufacture under Thomas Randall who had been important porcelain decorator in London. Evolved paste and ornament resembling then-popular old Sèvres. Bone china table ware from late 1830s.

Mahogany mainly from *c.* 1720; more from 1730s. 'Spanish', dark, hard-textured, straight grain, early, from San Domingo (141); 'Cuban' from *c.* 1740s, easier to work, with fiddle back and curl figure, especially for veneers; 'Honduras' or baywood, lighter, open grain, little figure and tending to fade, main variety for general furniture use in later 18th century.

Majolica, English (Note spelling: different from Italian maiolica.) From 1851 evolved by Herbert Minton: cane-coloured stoneware moulded in high relief and usually dipped in opaque white ground before firing, but with ornament depending on coloured glazes painted over this. Glowing tones of red, blue, pink, yellow, green, brown and so on. Some with mythological subjects adapted from Italian. Domestic English majolica from 1861 such as flower vases, bread trays, some using opaque colour glazes (268: Minton). From 1862 parian ware basis for some majolica figures, jugs. Wedgwood from *c.* 1861 included leaf plates (see *Green glaze ware*), with clear glazes on white body. Doulton from 1885, very strong, with colours over cream-coloured slip.

Manwaring, Robert at work 1760s as cabinet maker, chair maker and furniture designer whose *Cabinet and Chair Makers' Real Friend and Companion*, 1765, offered designs for chairs, garden seats and so on, including rustic work.

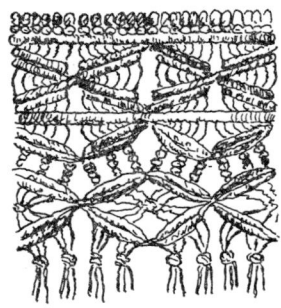

267 Macramé work detail

268 Majolica jug and chestnut dish by Mintons

269 Marbled neo-classic vase, Wedgwood

270 Typical ceramic marks: Bristol and Plymouth; Worcester; Derby; Minton; Swansea; Worcester

271 Marqueterie ware by Doulton

Maplewood Ancient use for veneers (praised by Pliny). In 1660s John Evelyn admired its grain 'when the knurs and nodosities are rarely diapered'. Edward Pinto has shown this to be the so-called mulberry of some distinctive burr veneers.

Maps Study of authentic specimens may help collector to recognise different qualities of hand-made paper and its watermarks, title cartouche treatment, symbols for towns, and so on, and border ornament, all of which changed down the centuries. Dates may be misleading as old printing plates were often altered and re-used. Many old maps are ruined by present-day colouring: collectors must recognise genuine contemporaneous colouring in tones of red lead, translucent willow green, crimson, gamboge, ultramarine and so on, slightly glazed with gum water.

Maps, embroidered In later 17th century might be printed on white satin. Minor vogue of *c.* 1770s when meticulously worked, sometimes over printed outlines, comparable with period's print-like embroidered pictures. Continued into Victorian days on fine canvas with names in cross stitch.

Marbled wares From 16th century in slipware; glaze marbling mainly later 18th century (**269**: Wedgwood); high temperature painted colours early 19th century. Colours intermingled on surface of ware in contrast to solid *agate ware* (q.v.). Wedgwood in 1770s evolved also imitations of granite, porphyry.

Marble mosaic Later 18th to later 19th centuries. Fragments of local marbles in range of subdued colours and mottlings cemented to tops of tables, first as 'scrap work', then as mosaic in conventional patterns and finally as birds and flowers. Mosaics eventually made in several regions but Derbyshire noted for more intricate inlay work, with the pieces fitting hollows chiselled in marble base (tables, snuff-boxes and so on).

Marbling, paper From mid-17th century. Book fore-edges from *c.* 1675 (see *fore-edge painting*). Popular wall coverings in 18th century and long used for book end-papers (**181**). Pattern created in colours on surface of trough of liquid size, elaborated if required with wooden comb. Sheet of unsized paper laid over it takes up colour with film of size. Finally polished, burnished.

Marks, ceramic Incised, painted or transfer-printed, usually under base. May indicate:

maker's name; date of firm's establishment (not of that piece's manufacture); pattern number (often mistaken for date); pattern title (365) (also confusing when it is, e.g. 'Dresden'); details of the design's registration (see *Registration marks*). Often merely copies of famous firms' marks, either contemporaneous or recently added. (270: Bristol and Plymouth; Worcester–formerly attributed to Caughley; Derby, Bloor; Minton; Swansea; Worcester.)

Marqueterie ware From *c*. 1886. Doulton. Tunbridge ware marquetry principles applied to earthenware, decoration built up with slices cut from blocks of coloured clays (271).

Marquetry Late 17th to early 18th century; 1770s–1780s; (272, 317); Victorian. Flat patterns glued upon surface of furniture created by cutting and exactly fitting together fragments of wood veneer in different colours or tones. Pattern and background might be cut together. In 19th-century wood often dyed or tinted. See also *Sand burning, Tunbridge ware*.

Marriage souvenirs Include: pair of knives in sheath; pewter vessels with initials arranged in triangle, surname at top with first names of husband and wife left and right below; chest with two sets of initials; fan with appropriate pictorial motifs; ceramic loving cup with individually painted names and date (264). But many fakes.

Marrow scoop From late 17th century. Silver, Sheffield plate, electro-plate. Spoon with narrow, elongated bowl and with still narrower flute as upper part of handle (273). Either end used for extracting marrow from beef bones, long popular delicacy. Sometimes ordinary spoon with marrow scoop handle.

Martin Brothers Four brothers covering period 1845–1923. Own studio pottery from

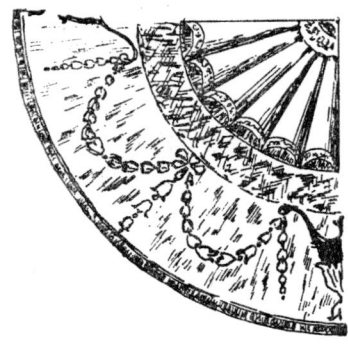

272 Marquetry ornament on pier table top, 1780s

273 Marrow scoop

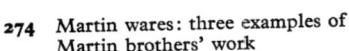

274 Martin wares: three examples of Martin brothers' work

275 Mary Gregory style of ornament on moulded glass

276 Mazer

1873; at Southall Pottery, 1877–1915. Achieved new colour effects, inlays and crackle finish with salt-glazed stoneware. Mainly ornamental wares, including grotesques **(274)**, double-face jugs. Many pieces signed and some dated.

Mary Gregory glass From *c.* 1870. Imitation of English *cameo glass* (q.v.) with ornament merely painted in white enamels on surface of clear or tinted glass vessels **(275)**. Supposedly named after one decorator doing such work at Boston & Sandwich Glass Co., Massachusetts, 1870s–80s. Imitations now abundant with poorly painted detail such as hands; sometimes tinted faces.

Mask Relief ornament in form of stylised face, human, lion, satyr. Found, e.g. carved on early Georgian table apron; as casting on neo-classic silver; as moulding under lip of jug **(56, 268, 368, 492)**; under string rim of *bellarmine* (q.v.); or developed into celebrity or character jug or mug. See also *Rodney*.

Mason ware Patented (1813) form of slightly translucent earthenware. See also *Ironstone china*. Included famous octagonal jugs with reptile handles in sets of three to fourteen, their heights $2\frac{1}{2}$–12 inches. Also fireplaces, five-foot-tall vases and on so.

Mazarine Silver, Sheffield plate, pewter, earthenware. Flat perforated plate, fitting inside serving-dish. At first (silver) under individual dishes of made-up meats. But more widely from 1770s under fish, then served whole and carved at table.

Mazer Medieval and later, turned wooden bowl **(276)**. In early days most suitable wood was burr or excrescence on trunk of maple tree, finely mottled (old German *mase* – speckle). Was unavoidably shallow, so given deep silver rim. Important for its silver mounts.

Measures See *Weights and measures, Mutchkin*.

Medallion Especially from 1760s. Panel or tablet, usually oval or circular. Introduced in neo-classic ornament such as furniture carving, marquetry, painting. Also in Wedgwood jasper ware, glass, displaying bas-relief portrait, classical or mythological figure scene. See also *Cameo*.

Medallion fan Especially 1770–90. Neo-classic ornament incorporating three medallions suitably painted on fine silk; sometimes small jasper-ware cameos set in guards.

Melon fluting Especially early 18th and early 19th centuries. Silver. Rounded vertical corrugations to strengthen vessel against denting (**277, 362**).

Mendlesham chair 19th century. Associated with Suffolk area. Low-back variant of Windsor chair, with saddle seat, splayed legs. Double crest rail often enclosing ball ornament above pierced splat (**278**).

Mercury twist glass Especially 1740–60. In drinking-glass stem, thick corkscrew of air in especially high-quality glass suggesting brilliance of quicksilver.

Merese On drinking glass. Collar, like one or more flat buttons, connecting bowl and stem or occasionally stem and foot (**370**).

Mezzotint In England from 1660. Print in velvety halftones reproducing painter's brushwork. Metal plate roughened all over (so that it would print black) then scraped to reduce this roughness to varying degrees (burnished for highlights). Important for reproducing late 18th-century portrait paintings.

Miers, J. 1758–1821. Leading silhouettist, painting his profiles in black on card or white composition medallions with exquisitely delicate detail. Included silhouette jewellery. His early Leeds work is rare. Used printed labels giving address and price; some include his son. 'Miers & Field' labels were used subsequently by his son working with John Field.

Millefiori glass ornament Italian term – glass of a thousand flowers. Ancient Roman technique; English-made from 1840s (Bacchus and others) copying French. Glass rods were formed of different colours in concentric layers, varied with such details as ribbing. Discs sliced from a number of different rods were laid out on clear glass, haphazardly or in patterns and covered with more clear glass which fused imperceptibly, securing pattern in solid glass. For paper-weight, ink-bottle stopper, clear glass often shaped as dome which magnified and intensified pattern. Or a cushion of glass was cased (see also *cased glass*) in opaque colour and the pattern viewed in miniature through concavities ground through the casing (**279**).

Miniatures, painted Costume ornament from 16th century. Some by master artists but

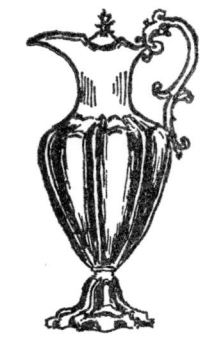

277 Melon fluting on silver jug

278 Mendlesham chair

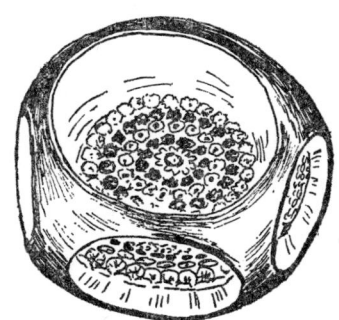

279 Millefiori work in cased glass paper-weight

280 Typical Minton pattern mark

281 Miser purse, closed and open

282 Mocha ware, jug and mug

283 Moneybox, earthenware, with crude hen and chicks

very many more by copyists, less perfect and unsigned for sitter to give away. Some early, in gouache, on vellum; paper, early 18th century; ivory ovals increasingly used through 18th century, being stipple-painted from *c.* 1730; on playing-cards mainly 19th century. Some in oil paint; in enamels mainly 18th-early 19th century.

Minton firm Stoke-on-Trent. Potters from 1789 onwards; Mintons from 1872. Thomas Minton (d. 1836) joined by son Herbert in 1817. Table wares, cabinet porcelains, parian statuary, English majolica, imitations of Palissy and Della Robbia wares; such ornamental techniques as flower encrustations, acid-gilding, pâte-sur-pâte, including work long attributed to Rockingham and Coalport. From 1842 marks **(270)** included small impressed year symbols. (**280**: shows inconspicuous M in pattern title).

Miser purse Now popular name for stocking purse in wide use from 18th century with central slit opening and 'toe' ends to hang down from hand or belt. Two metal rings could be slid from centre over slit to secure coins in the toes (**281**: closed and open). Made by knitting, crochet, buttonhole stitching, often incorporating glass, cut steel or gilt metal beads for longer wear and with appropriate tassel weight (gilded, silver, copper) on each end to indicate its contents.

Mitre Furniture. Diagonal line of junction where two mouldings or bands of veneer intersect at right angles, a detail expected of good quality English cabinet making **(214)**.

Mocha ware Mainly from 1790s onwards, for workaday table wares **(282)**, measures, spill vases. Decorated with bands of irregular ornament in fine wavering lines suggesting ferns, moss, trees, created by allowing prepared colour with acid base to diffuse through wet clay slip before glazing and firing.

Modeller, porcelain Maker of the original wax or clay figure required for shaping master mould. From this, working moulds were made, each for shaping in great numbers a different detail of the figure. Shaped parts were then assembled before firing, the craftsman responsible being known, confusingly, as a repairer.

Monarch's head silver mark 1784–1890. Included in row of hallmarks to indicate payment of silver duty. Changes in monarch aid dating but provincial assay offices might be slow in introducing new punches. Two impressions on work assayed 1797–8 when duty doubled.

Money box Christmas box, rattling box, used by Elizabethan and Georgian apprentices and houseboys. Earthenware vessel smashed to obtain contents: hence simple designs such as dome topped by crude hen and chicks **(283)**, barrel, pine-cone, bee-skip. Horizontal slits from later 17th century. Primitive designs continued into 19th century. Cottage shapes 19th century. Larger boxes for copper coin only from end of 18th century (cart-wheel twopenny pieces from 1797).

Monteith Silver, ceramics. From late 17th century. Bowl with notched or undulating rim, usually loose, to hold ice water for cooling wine glasses supported from rim by their feet **(284)**. Leeds (cream ware) called them glass trays.

Moons, porcelain Small areas of exceptional translucency due to imperfect mixing of ingredients seen when held against light in some early soft-paste porcelain, e.g. of Chelsea, Bow.

Moorfields carpets From *c.* 1760 made by Thomas Moore at Moorfields, London. Loosely hand-knotted in Turkish manner. Design included commissions from Robert Adam.

Morris, William 1834–96. Major designer and contributor to late 19th-century arts and crafts; friend of Pre-Raphaelite artists; founder of firm Morris, Marshall, Faulkner & Co. in 1861, 'fine art workmen in painting, carving, furniture and the metals'. Enthusiasm for romantic medievalism included fabric patterns, carpets, printed books (Merton Abbey Tapestry Works, Kelmscott Press). He did not personally design any furniture but is associated with two designs **(285)** popular from 1860s.

Mortar (1) Common Middle Ages to end of 18th century. Heavy bowl-shape vessel of stone **(286)**, bronze, marble, pewter, wood **(253)** for use with club-shaped pestle by apothecary and cook, to pound or bruise substances. (2) Open-bowl lamp with floating wick. (3) 19th-century slow-burning, thick candle for night-light.

Mortise-and-tenon joint From late 15th century. In furniture for right-angle joining of rails in chairs, chests, stools **(236)** and so on. Groove cut in side of wood fitted tongue projecting from end, the joint held firm by

284 Monteith, silver, late 17th century

285 'Morris' chairs

286 Mortar of stone, with pestle above

287 Mortise-and-tenon joint: two views of stool foot and stretcher arrangement

288 Mote skimmer, 1750s

289 Mother of pearl ware (Belleek)

290 Mounts on Sheffield plate inkstand, 1820s

wooden *dowel pin* (q.v.), driven through both members **(287)**.

Mortlock, J. and successors 1746–*c.* 1930. Celebrated London china sellers and decorators. During 19th century were agents for Coalport, Derby, Minton, Wedgwood and Worcester. Name often found along with maker's mark: style and address may aid dating **(118)**. From 1893 firm was Mortlocks Ltd.

Mosaics See *Marble, Paper mosaic, Tunbridge ware.*

Mote skimmer Silver. 18th century. Detail of fashionable tea equipage. Long teaspoon with decoratively pierced bowl and its finial shaped as tiny barb **(288)**. The bowl skimmed dust floating on poured cup of tea and finial cleared leaves choking teapot spout-strainer.

Mother of pearl Innermost iridescent lining of various conch and bi-valve shells. 16th–17th centuries: mosaics of pearly shell riveted over silverware; stemmed vessels made of nautilus shells (much reproduced by Victorians). 17th century: some furniture inlay. 18th century: as knife handles, games counters (English or Oriental engraved), pierced and foil-decorated Georgian fan sticks **(163)**. 19th century: vastly popular for card cases **(470)**, tea caddies, paper knives, and so on, including less lustrous, thicker Australian shell. Trade increased from late 1830s, shell for inlay being ground instead of filed.

Mother of pearl encrustation From mid-1820s popular ornament on papier mâché, known as inlay **(310)**. Glued on surface and levelled with more background varnish. From 1840s shell ground paper-thin and shaped and etched with acid. Used, e.g. in pictorial scenes, some overpainted in clear colour.

Mother of pearl ware English patent 1857 by Frenchman, J. J. Brianchon, for iridescent glaze based on resin, given shell-like gleam with gold chloride. This used on parian ware at Belleek Pottery, County Fermanagh, for vessels with marine ornament **(34, 289)**, flower encrustations, openwork baskets. Glaze, slightly modified, used by Worcester; W. H. Goss; S. Moore; Herbert Minton; W. T. Copeland. Much ware issued unmarked.

Mounts Metal ornaments, rims, feet, to protect vulnerable parts of furniture, ceramics and other fragile wares. Essential for hinged rims of many boxes – in materials such as painted enamels (**40**, **158**), tortoiseshell, hard-stones.

Mounts, Sheffield plate To keep line of copper core from showing at cut edges. At first, merely sheared and silver pressed over copper. From *c.* 1768 ribbon of flattened plated wire soldered on; 1775–1815, wire in U-section, of silver. From *c.* 1780 some high-quality work with solid silver cast mounts finished with hand chasing; from early 1790s, silver mounts shaped by stamping and filled with lead-tin alloy in bead, thread, gadroon patterns, becoming wider, more decorative from 1815 (**290**), improved 1824. Some *electrotype* (q.v.) mounts from mid-1840s.

291 Muffineer

Muffineer Silver and imitations. 1760s–Victorian. For sprinkling cinnamon on toasted muffins. Small stemmed castor, baluster shape with tall domed cover (**291**). 1780s, lower dome; from 1790s some cylindrical; some pierced and blue-lined. Many designs returned in Victorian period.

Mug Individual-handled drinking vessel comparable with can but distinguished by inclusion of base rim and hence needing no saucer. Fascinating to collect because found in every kind of ceramic from porcelain (**260**) and cabinet china to earthenware (**282**) and salt-glazed stoneware; also silver (**319**), pewter and so on. Changing shapes indicate period (**292**: Stuart to Victorian).

Mule chest 17th century. Modern term for joiner's first attempt to cater for separate storage. Indiscriminate box-space of chest augmented by one or two full-width drawers, forerunner of chest entirely divided into drawers.

292 Mugs, earthenware, in date sequence, Stuart to Victorian

Musical box From 1800s, weak-toned and liable to chatter. Series of improvements from *c.* 1820 such as feather-quill dampers from *c.* 1825; loud-and-soft movement, 1838; mandoline tones from *c.* 1840; drum and bell notes from *c.* 1850 (visible from *c.* 1860 and common in cheaper boxes from 1875). Flute effects from *c.* 1850. Mechanism for changing the music cylinders, 1854. Cheaper manufacturing methods from 1883–5. Changing tastes also traceable in box treatment and choice of music. See also *Automata*.

Mutchkin Pewter. Scottish measure, three-quarters of Imperial pint (**293**); larger versions were chopin and tappit hen, the latter one Scottish or three imperial measure pints.

293 Mutchkin, pewter

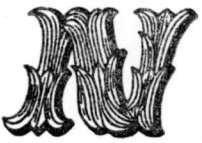

294 Nailsea glass: rolling pin, bell, 'bellows' bottle. See also 195.

Nailsea glass Nailsea Glasshouse near Bristol worked 1788–1873 but term covers types made also at Sunderland, Newcastle, Stourbridge, Warrington, Alloa and elsewhere. Jugs, rolling-pins (294) and much imitative ornament such as giant tobacco pipes (52), in low-taxed bottle glass, dark and pale green, patterned with contrasting streaks and surface crimping. Full colour flint-glass widely made after tax lifted, 1845 but not at Nailsea. See also *Coloured glass*.

Nantgarw porcelain Established 1813 by renowned porcelain decorator *William Billingsley* (q.v.) who moved to Swansea 1814 but returned to Nantgarw 1817, making very fine flatware until 1820 (295: painted ornament). Soft paste, very white, highly translucent with lustrous glaze.

Needle-case Medieval pocket hanging from girdle to hold bronze needles, long continued. By 18th–19th centuries, customary steel needles usually in moisture-resistant cylindrical screw-cap case (459) of wood or bone covered in shagreen, fine beadwork, Tunbridge mosaic, or of carved ivory, piqué-worked tortoiseshell, mother-of-pearl. Included imitation shapes (bellows, quiver of arrows, parasol, pea-pod). In 19th century development of shallow rectangular needle-box to hold papers of needles in graded sizes and covered, e.g. with *Baxter* (q.v.) 'needleprints'. But many late Victorians preferred needlebooks and combated rust with emery cushions.

Needlepoint lace From 16th century, evolving from drawn thread embroidery. Distinguished from lighter, cheaper bobbin lace by being created with needle and single continuous thread, using loop or buttonhole stitch (47), instead of intertwisting numerous threads. Called parchment lace in 17th century because worked over parchment pattern.

295 Nantgarw porcelain, painted detail

Nef From 13th century, but mainly silver imports. Ceremonial ship model for dining-table, in precious metals set with jewels for head of noble household to contain personal salts, spices, knives and so on. From c. 16th century English work included smaller vessels. From later 17th century on wheels instead of pedestal and used for serving wine (**296**: early 18th-century). From later 18th century, less costly, English and Dutch, as table centre-pieces for sweetmeats. Most now found are 19th-century intended as wine coolers or bottle coasters.

296 Nef, early 18th century

Neo-classic style Popularised in England from c. 1760 by Robert Adam and applied to contemporaneous furnishings; around 1800 heavier-handed archaeological approach attempting to recreate classical designs. Well-proportioned flowing curves, straight tapering legs (**317, 323, 357**), urn and vase shapes, Graeco-Roman ornament – patera (**315**), honeysuckle (**9**), husk, reeding, fluting (**297**).

297 Neo-classic style, three examples in silver, furniture

Netting Especially 17th–18th centuries and mid-Victorian. Hobby for men (William Morris as a boy) and women. Wide range of quality from garden nets to basis for embroidery, using 'needle' with U-shaped slits. Netting box, fashionable late 18th century, included roller for made net. See also *Knotting* and *Tatting*.

New Hall, Shelton 1781– c. 1830, making hard porcelain (wet-looking glaze) until c. 1810 and thereafter bone china. Remembered for silver-shape teapot (**298**), with feet instead of loose stand from c. 1800. Hand-painted ornament until 1800 then some transfer-printing. Early mark was cursive *N*; on bone china *New Hall* encircled.

Nickel silver Like german silver, containing no silver. Alloy of zinc and nickel with a

298 New Hall porcelain teapot

299 Nottingham ware loving cup

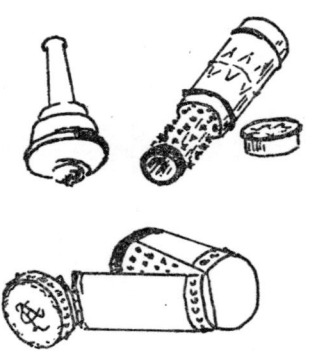

300 Nutmeg graters (pocket) including 'mace' (*top left*)

little copper, used from 1840s as basis for electro-plating with **EPNS** mark.

Niello From medieval days and especially 16th and 19th centuries. Black compound (lead, silver, copper, sulphur) heated in muffle kiln, used to fill and hence emphasise engraved ornament on metal.

Night light Earthenware, bone china. Mainly popular from 1830s for improved slow-burning, non-guttering candle. Included models of cottages, churches with window holes and designs where light shone through ornamental panel such as *lithophane* (q.v.) or mother of pearl.

Nonsuch chest Late 16th–early 17th centuries, probably work of immigrant German or Flemish craftsmen. Inlay ornament composed of variously coloured woods showing buildings somewhat resembling (a) prints of Henry VIII's Nonsuch Palace; (b) timber-built Nonsuch House on London Bridge.

Nottingham lace From early 19th century, especially from expiry of Heathcote patent, 1823. Net patterned in imitation of bobbin lace, woven by machinery. Full range by Jacquard patent from 1837, tending to be flimsy, weak-edged, merely woven or twisted, lacking plaited stitches.

Nottingham stoneware 1690s–1800s. Brown salt-glazed, with smooth surface of clay slip containing iron oxide, evolved by James Morley. Intensely rich brown tones with slight metallic lustre. Jugs, teapots, mugs, often with incised **(299)** and stamped ornament; also double-wall perforated vessels. Name soon applied to similar but inferior ware from Derbyshire.

Nutmeg grater Silver, Sheffield plate. From late 17th century but mainly 1770s–1830s, for hot toddy. Pocket size **(300)** shaped as cylinder (with tubular grater); box (hinged, in heart shape or oval); egg shape, opened by unscrewing (larger after 1790); urn shape hinged at foot from *c.* 1780. Grater: silver with uneven holes, pre-1740; hammered sheet steel, to 1770s; *blued steel* (q.v.).

Oak Heavy brown wood familiar in early framed-up, *joined furniture* (q.v.). From 16th century much imported as clapboard or wainscot – whiter, more easily worked than the slow-growing English oak used for ships, houses. Early manner of splitting wood made most of familiar hard-surfaced *silver grain* (q.v.).

Oeil de perdrix (partridge eye). 18th–19th-century painted ornament on porcelain; small circular spots of colour, each surrounded by ring of smaller dots. Madeley, Minton and others in Sèvres manner **(301)**.

301   *Oeil de perdrix* porcelain ornament

Ogee Glass, furniture, term for somewhat S-shaped double curve flowing smoothly downwards from concave to convex. Frequent outline for drinking-glass bowls – and double-ogee – **(150, 302)** and for cabinet furniture moulding.

Old Hall, Hanley From 1770, address of Job Meigh and successors, making high quality earthenwares. From 1830s, stone china; from 1840s ambitious 'Gothic' pictorial jugs **(200)**. From 1861 firm was Old Hall Earthenware Co.; 1887–1902 Old Hall Porcelain Co.

302   Ogee and double ogee outlines in wine and sweetmeat glasses

Oleograph Late 19th century. From Germany, used by, e.g. firm of William Dickes. Chromolithograph varnished and passed under roller to give surface texture suggesting oil-painting on canvas.

Ombre table From 17th century. Three-sided, for game brought to England from Spain by Charles II's Queen Catherine.

Omnium, whatnot From 1790s. Furniture. Stand of three or four open shelves supported on corner columns such as turned spindles or carved scrolls. Mahogany, rosewood, later walnut. For displaying ornaments accessible from all sides and often protected by low

303   Omnium, Victorian

304 Opaline glass, painted and hung with Victorian lustres

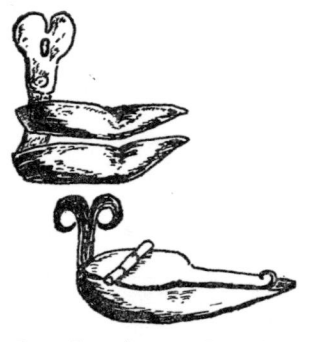

305 Open-flame lamps – Betty lamp and spout lamp

306 Orders: clock and candlestick adaptations of Tuscan and Corinthian columns

brass fret galleries. From 1840s in wide use (**303**); from *c.* 1855 included triangular designs, the front of each shelf often in a cyma curve.

Opaline glass Early Victorian. Opacified with phosphate of lime at a period delighting in range of semi-opaque glass – pearline, pearl-opal and so on, a fashion including also cornelian, topaz, vaseline, even chrysoprase glass. Not cut, but surface ornamented with clear colour reliefs (flowers, reptiles), gilding, painting (**304**: mantelpiece ornament hung with glass lustres).

Opaque china, opaque porcelain From early 19th century, terms used by Swansea and many Victorian potters for improved felspathic earthenwares – sturdy, workaday improvements on stone china, pure white, somewhat translucent, with clear ringing tone. Much decorated underglaze. Granite ware from late 1850s.

Opaque glass From 1750s onwards, suggesting white porcelain. Opacified with tin oxide; from 1780s, more cheaply with arsenic. See *Enamel glass, Lime-soda-potash glass, Opaline glass.*

Opaque twist stem Mid 1740s–80s on drinking glass. Threads of white enamel glass spiralling down centre of clear-glass stem.

Open-flame lamps Slut was primitive hanging bowl with flat floating wick. Crusie was improvement with pinched spout for wick; 17th century, drip-catching double crusie or Betty lamp (**305 top**). Lidded spout lamp (**305 bottom**) from 1720s with iron wick-prick chained to lid. Ribbon wicks from 1760s. Argand lamp (**246 right**) with tubular wick for better air supply from 1780s; Liverpool lamp from 1800s with adjustable light; moderator lamp with controlled oil flow from 1830s. Dangerous benzine from 1825; paraffin from 1861, ending traditional open flame lamp design. See also *Lamps.*

Orders Interest revived with Renaissance and applied more intelligently from 17th century. Furniture, silver. Classic system governing proportions in architectural design: Doric, Ionic, Corinthian (Greek) and Tuscan and Composite (Roman). (**306, 480**: adaptations of Tuscan and Corinthian; **324**: Doric.) Can be traced in much pillar work on cabinets, candlesticks and so on. Entablature (cornice, frieze and architrave), sometimes surmounted by pediment, rested on distinctively shaped capital, column and base.

Ormolu 18th–19th centuries. Term originated from use of powdered leaf gold (*or moulu*) to gild bronze. Became usual term for mounts – handles, corner ornaments (**194, 307**) and so on – cast in a refined golden-coloured alloy composed mainly of zinc and copper, gilded to protect from tarnish. *Matthew Boulton* (q.v.) leading English manufacturer.

Overlay glass See *Cased glass*.

Ovolo moulding Furniture. Simple finish to fill angle between mouldings; convex so that its section is quarter-circle.

Oyster veneer From late 17th century. On cabinet furniture, symmetrical pattern on surface created with almost-identical pieces of veneer cut from tree branch showing marked concentric rings, such as laburnum (**308**).

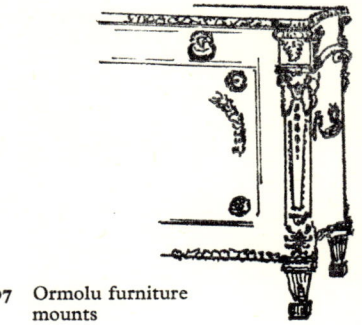

307 Ormolu furniture mounts

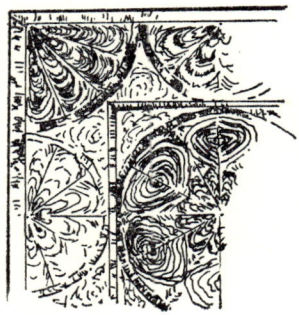

308 Oyster veneer

309 Paper weight, Sowerby pressed glass

Palladian style English vogue named after 16th-century Italian Palladio. Austere classic design in architecture (as relief from robust baroque) interpreted in magnificently-planned interiors, marble pillars, stucco ornament, sumptuous furnishings, somewhat ponderous furniture. See also *William Kent*.

Panel Furniture. Rectangle of thin wood framed by thicker vertical and horizontal *rails* (q.v.); usually slightly sunk or projecting. Sometimes square or elliptical. Typical of oak construction, as in front of chest. Term panelling implies panels and their framing. Changing styles aid dating.

Paper mosaic From 18th century, hobby prompted by a few professionals who knife-cut portraits, coats of arms, in vellum. From 1773 *Mrs. Delany* (q.v.) set example by composing nearly 1,000 botanically exact flower sprays (now in British Museum) to suggest pressed flowers. Each different tone and shadow required separate wisp cut from suitable coloured paper bought from paper-stainers and stuck down on thick black paper, their details overlapping to aid three-dimensional effect.

Paper-ware Patented 1772 by Henry Clay, making trays, tea-caddy panels, stronger than *papier mâché* (q.v.). Sheets of paste-saturated linen-rag overlaid to required thickness, hand-shaped over moulds, stove-dried, layer by layer until extremely hard; coloured with opaque varnishes stove-dried and hand polished. Clay succeeded 1816 by *Jennens & Bettridge* (q.v.).

Paper-weights Many Victorian fancies such as realistic animals, reptiles, fruits, human hands, in metals, ceramics, hard stones and so on. In glass **(309)** range from bottle-glass domes enclosing air bubbles to splendid *crystal cameos* and bun-shaped *millefiori* (q.v.)

310 Papier mâché: M'Cullum & Hodgson chair

Papier mâché In production from before

mid-18th century – much earlier for interior decoration. From *c.* 1830s name in general use for pulp of rag, paper and gum, a quicker, cheaper form of paper-ware. Richard Brindley developed press-die shaping, results being less perfectly smooth but still warp-free, glossy. Included small furniture, boxes, screens, card cases and so on (**311**, **497**). Impressed marks on paper-ware and papier mâché include M'Cullum & Hodgson (**310**) and Jennens & Bettridge (**311**) Birmingham, and Wolverhampton firms of Alderman, Illidge, Shoolbred & Loveridge, Edward Perry, F. Walton & Co., A. Morton & Co.

Papier mâché ornament Applied over stove-hardened surface of japan varnish (**311**: design by Richard Redgrave for Jennens & Bettridge, see *Summerly's Art Manufactures*). Fadeless black from 1830s. Early gold borders followed by glittering bronze powders, patented 1812. Romantic 'Wolverhampton' style with moonlight scenes, Gothic church windows (**66**). Pearl-shell encrustations patented 1825; acid-shaped shell from 1840. Flowers especially 1830s–40s, sea-shells 1840s, ferns 1850s and imitations of malachite, agate, even wood veneers.

Parcel gilt Silverware partially gilded.

Parian ware From 1842 by Copeland & Garrett and others, especially Minton firm. Form of highly vitrified porcelain (feldspar and china clay), ivory white with surface suggesting parian marble. Many mid-Victorian busts, figures shaped in quantity from moulds but suggesting individual sculpture and frequently bearing name of sculptor who made original model.

Parian ware, domestic From late 1840s. Cheaper variant, finished with smear-glazing. Much used for relief-ornamented jugs (**312**) and vases.

Parquetry From 1660s. Furniture. Matching veneers forming symmetrical geometrical patterns (**313**).

Pastille burner, ceramic From *c.* 1700 onwards in slip-ware; mingled-colour 'Whieldon' from 1750s; Bristol hard porcelain 1770s (**314**: Chamberlain). But found today mainly in bone china from 1820s, including many *flower-encrusted cottages* (q.v.), summerhouses, castles. Slowly smouldering pastilles (charcoal, gum benzoin, aromatic oils) perfumed many Victorian living-rooms.

311   Papier mâché ornament: Jennens & Bettridge supper tray

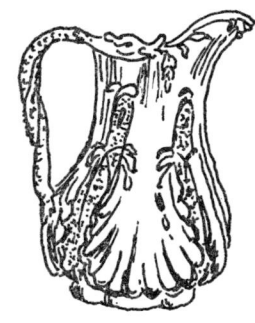

312   Parian ware, relief ornamented jug

313   Parquetry: corner of card table

314   Pastille burner in Chamberlain porcelain

315 Patera furniture ornament

Patch box Serving 17th–18th-century fashion. Small shallow box characterised by steel mirror inside lid. Fascinating range of ornamental materials and fine metal mounts. Often pull-off lid, in contrast to hinged snuff-box. But probably many so-called were intended for comfits. See also *Bonbonnières* and *Comfitholders*.

Patchwork Recorded from Mediaeval days; exist mainly from late 18th–19th centuries. Bed covers, cushions and other furnishings composed of small pieces of different fabrics cut to geometric shapes and edge-joined. Background fabric only for strength, not visible from front. Delicately-patterned fabrics especially 1800s–30s. Some centrepieces (c. 1800–20) printed for the purpose, sometimes commemorative with date. Hexagonal pieces especially from 1850s; also use of glossy silk to emphasise outlines. Some Victorian pictorial patchwork; also autographed album quilts. Irregularly-pieced crazy quilts were late Victorian disaster. See also *Appliqué work* and *Quilting*.

Patera Especially 1760s onwards. Furniture (**315, 440**), metals. Saucer-shaped ornament with concentric pattern flat or in low relief. In Adam design and much used whenever neo-classic style was in vogue.

Pâte-sur-pâte Ancient technique. English from *c.* 1870. Ceramic ornament associated with mid-19th-century Sèvres and introduced to Mintons by M. L. Solon. Semi-translucent watery clay slip was painted over coloured ground, successive layers with tool-sculptured detail achieving subtle gradations of tone from intense white, where slip thickest, to shadows coloured by underlying ground. Finished with glaze and gilding. Comparable with some cameo glass.

Patina Surface texture and tone on long-cared-for furniture. Also bloom or film on surface of old bronze due to oxidisation.

Pattern numbers, ceramics Often the only marks and not to be mistaken for dates. Mainly on useful wares. Most firms used consecutive numbers into thousands. Some then began again at 1 but with a letter or figure prefix (e.g. Grainger X from 1839, Copeland D from 1852, Rockingham 2). Others used a figure on top of the number (Grainger from 1845, Coalport).

Pearl ware From 1779. Evolved by Wedgwood. Not iridescent. Misleading term for

316 Pedlar doll

white earthenware containing more calcined flint and china clay than cream-coloured earthenware which it largely replaced. Yellowish tinge removed by 1790. See also *Mother of pearl ware*.

Pedlar doll From late 18th century. Necessarily fixed on stand so that tray, bearing hawker's licence, could be filled with tiny articles, originally often specialised stock such as jewellery, household goods, even tiny printed broadsheets **(316)**. Usually woman in bonnet and red cloak or Victorian plaid shawl. Sometimes early Victorian man and woman pair: market man and woman may be labelled Whites of Milton, Portsmouth. Many reproductions with modern trinkets.

Peg tankard 17th-century vessel for communal drinking containing vertical line of studs to serve as measure. Genuine specimens rare.

Pellatt, Apsley, M.P. 1791–1863. Enterprising Londoner (responsible among other reforms for making crossed cheque payable only through bank), author of *Curiosities of Glassmaking*, 1849. Developed wide range of plaques, paperweights, decanters, trinkets at Falcon Glassworks, Southwark. See also *Crystal cameo*.

Pembroke table From *c.* 1750s. Light breakfast table with small falling flaps supported on fly brackets intended to look well when flaps down. Open top usually squarish-rectangle often with rounded corners **(317**: Hepplewhite design) – occasionally elliptical – contrasting with *sofa table's* long narrow top and falling ends.

Pennington, Seth Established early 1780s. Notable Liverpool maker of soft-paste porcelain, often with relief ornament.

Penwork Late 18th–early 19th centuries. Surface ornament for japanned cabinets, table tops, described by Sheraton as imitation of etching. Surface was japanned black then hand-painted with all-over design in white japan, given finer definition with quill-pen work in Indian ink **(318**: cabinet and pattern detail).

Petal fluting Each channel ends in arching curve **(319)** – opposite of *bat's-wing fluting* (q.v.).

Petitpoint embroidery Mainly from mid-16th century onwards. Tent stitch **(115 bottom)**, not to be confused with coarser

317 Pembroke table (design from Hepplewhite's *Guide*)

318 Penwork cabinet and detail of typical ornament

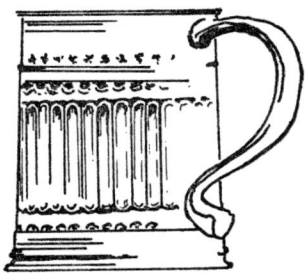

319 Petal fluting on silver tankard

cross-stitch (q.v.). Consists of rows of close diagonal stitches, a single stitch over each crossing of warp and weft thread of fabric. Worked with backward slant, reinforcing back of work and giving great strength to usual linen ground which is entirely covered. Firescreens, bags, book covers, important panels on furniture.

Pew group From c. 1730s. Figure group consisting of woman and one or two men, often with musical instruments, on high-backed settle (no religious significance). Hand-modelled primitive figures in salt-glazed stoneware, white with dark clay detail (**14**). Some in lead-glazed earthenware with touches of colour. Many reproductions.

320 Pewter candlesticks, 17th, 18th and 19th centuries

Pewter (**143**, **235**: tankards; **252**, **293**: measures; **320**: candlesticks, 17th, 18th, 19th centuries.) From 14th century strict rules of Pewterers' Company specified qualities of pewter: *sadware*, *trifle* and *ley metal* (see separate entries). From mid-18th century leadless pewter reintroduced. See also *Britannia metal* and *Vickers metal*.

Picture ribbons Patented 1862. Detailed, vividly coloured glossy silk pictorial work – portraits, sporting scenes, topical events and so on – created by loom weaving, first as 6–9 in. book markers; later valentines, Christmas ribbons and other souvenirs. Made famous by Thomas Stevens, Coventry, established 1854. See *Stevengraph*. Other makers, in colour or print-like black and white, included W. H. Grant who showed at 1885 International Exhibition, Odell & French, Ratcliff & Son and J. Hart.

321 Piecrust table

Picture trays From late 18th century and especially through early 19th, in iron or paper ware or papier mâché in range of named shapes – flat-rimmed sandwich, kidney, gadroon-edged Gothic, scallop-bordered Albert and more deeply indented Victoria. Painted ornament by skilled factory copyists after Gainsborough, Morland and others. Many coaching scenes, religious groups, birds.

Piecrust table Popular around 1760. Top following silver design of 1720s–30s. Modern name for *pillar-and-claw* (q.v.) table with its top turned in repetitive cyma outline of contrasting straight and curved sections (**321**). Low inch-wide rim suggests crimping of pastry. Many reproductions, often circular without regard for the slight cross-grain shrinkage of genuine antiques.

322 Piecrust ware

Piecrust ware, crock pies From end of 18th century to later 19th. *Cane-ware* (q.v.) lidded vessels shaped and decorated to resemble elaborate standing pies during wartime flour restrictions. Made by Wedgwood (**322**), Davenport, J. & W. Turner, Samuel Hollins, E. Mayer & Son, Charles Meigh and others. In 1792–6 Lakin & Poole invoiced English pies and French pies. Moulded specimens, less sharply detailed, by J. & W. Ridgway from mid-1830s. Cheap heat-resistant oven wares from *c.* 1850 made in Derbyshire (Woodville, Swadlincote and so on, including Denby 'pork pie' crusts as late as 1870s in cane stoneware). Wedgwood to compete made glazed ironstone oven dishes to fit inside terracotta piecrusts.

323 Pier table (Sheraton design)

Pier glass, pier table From 18th century. Usually in pairs. Long, narrow mirror in elaborate gilded frame hanging over D-shaped or semi-elliptical table in each pier or wall-space between windows in formal Georgian room (**323**: Sheraton pier table design).

Pilasters Architectural motifs on furniture. Columns attached along their length to the piece of furniture they decorate, such as front corners of chest of drawers (**324**: 1750s, 1800s, 1840s).

324 Pilasters, 1750s, 1800s, 1840s

Pilgrim bottle See *Costrel*.

Pillar-and-claw furniture From 18th century, popular construction for small tables (**321**), firescreens, dumb waiters. Three short cabriole legs projecting from and dovetailed into base of pillar which is usually ornamentally turned, sometimes more expensively carved (**325**).

Pillow lace Created by twisting and intermingling a number of threads (wound on bobbins) with aid of pins stuck in small padded pillow (**47 top**). Alternative to the technique of

325 Pillar-and-claw teapoy

326 Pincushions: beadwork, and pin ornament (*left*); table clamp, and watch
shape (*centre*); Tunbridge ware (*right*)

single-thread stitches used in needlepoint lace.
Includes *bobbin lace, bone lace* (q.v.). Machine-
made 'flowered net' from *c.* 1770 but mainly
developed from 1809. See also *Nottingham lace.*

Pill slab Ceramic. Flat slab of tin-enamelled
earthenware used by apothecaries for mixing
and rolling pills. Commonly blue painted;
occasionally used by a member of the Society
of Apothecaries to declare the fact by displaying Company's arms.

Pinchbeck Early 18th-century invention of
alloy more nearly imitating gold than ordinary
brass. This depended on quality of its copper
and zinc and finishing process to give golden
tone. Used for articles kept tarnish-free by
constant use and pocket-friction. Watchmaker
Christopher Pinchbeck passed secret to son
who advertised wide range of bijouterie, 1733–
47. Name soon applied to inferior forms of
brass, cheaply gilded, used by Birmingham
makers of buckles, boxes, costume jewellery.

Pinched glass 18th–19th centuries. Small
solid glass units such as decanter stoppers
supplied to larger glassworks. Shaped by
specialist small-scale glassmen using hand
tools and known as pinchers. Vases, candlesticks and so on may show different quality of
glass in such units as feet.

Pinched plate Popular 16th–17th centuries.
Silver wire flattened by wire-drawers to produce narrow metal ribbon for professional
embroidery. Substantial enough to give rich
gleam among massed seed pearls, wire purls,
bugles stitched on to wear-resistant book
covers, glove gauntlets, sword belts.

Pincushion From Medieval days, capped
cylinder of silver, ivory, wood – pin poppet –
protected hand-wrought iron pins. Remaining
pincushions include many gifts, late 17th to

327 Pinxton (typical mark *above*)

early 19th centuries, stuck with pins spelling wedding or birthday greetings (**326 bottom left**). Skimpy Regency fashions required flat designs such as double discs rimmed with pins; and flat imitative outlines – wheelbarrow, swan, watch (**326 bottom centre**) – in mother of pearl and so on. Victorians included patchwork, dolls, silver birds and other imitative shapes (**326 right**: Tunbridge ware) and innumerable massive cushions buttoned, braided, fringed. Emery filling for sharpening points and removing rust.

Pineapple ware See *Cauliflower ware*.

Pinewood Especially from 1660s onwards as easily worked basis or carcase for veneers. When pale the wood was known as yellow deal; when reddish, as red deal or pine. Pitch pine, yellow, resinous, popular 19th century for church and school furniture.

Pinxton Small, short-lived porcelain factory in Derbyshire making porcelain 1796–9 and later bone china. Ornament includes views of country mansions, landscapes (**327**: with mark above) and the popular *Chantilly sprig* (q.v.) Founded by *William Billingsley* (q.v.).

Piqué In England from late 17th century but no equivalent English name. Tortoiseshell or ivory patterned with tiny studs of gold or silver set into the surface and polished into smooth radiance. Fan sticks, snuff-boxes, knife handles, cane heads (**328 left**), watch cases. A heavier version was known as nailhead piqué; substantial inlays of strip gold were *posé d'or* (**328 right**).

Plate Wrought gold or silver which, when British, usually bears appropriate hallmarks. Not to be confused with Sheffield plate (silver heat-fused over copper) or electro-plate (silver thinly deposited over copper or a nickel alloy).

Plate mark Any print produced by intaglio process, such as line engraving, requires great pressure on the damp paper in the printing press. Whole surface of paper retains mark of contact with the prepared metal plate, being distinctly lower than its surrounding margins.

Plate pail 18th–19th centuries. Brass-mounted mahogany bucket, round or polygonal, with straight sides containing narrow slit, top to bottom (**329**). For carrying plates between kitchens and dining-room.

Playing-cards From medieval days. From 1712 to 1862 may be dated by excise tax marks

328 Piqué: parasol handle, earring, etui (*posé d'or*) and shuttle-shaped box

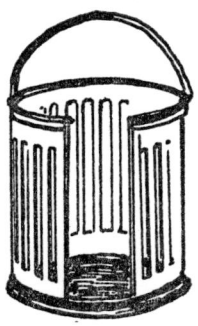

329 Plate pail

330 Plymouth hard-paste porcelain

printed over ace of spades (see *Duty ace*). Until 1840 backs usually plain. Figure indices from 1862; with letters from 1884. Rounded corners from 1862. Double-headed court cards from 1867.

Plymouth porcelain Established 1768, after William Cookworthy discovered, patented and thus monopolised Cornish stone and china clay for the first English hard-paste porcelain **(48, 330)**. Moved to Bristol 1770 (Mark **270**).

Poker work 18th century and more especially early Victorian amateur ornament, formal and pictorial, worked on minor wooden furniture with hot skewers, the charred wood being removed by rubbing with sand **(331)**. Professional work in relief by such firms as the Burnwood Carving Co.

Pole screen 18th–19th centuries. Attractively slender firescreen with plain stem rising from claw or tripod feet to support adjustable screen often framing embroidery. Some early walnut; mainly mahogany **(332**: showing back adjustment screw). More substantial in early 19th century. Some, Victorian, of painted copper or papier mâché; elaborately carved wood around 1850.

Pomander Mainly 15th–16th centuries as protection from ill-odours and disease. Gold or silver, jewelled or enamelled, openwork ball, about 1 in. across, containing ambergris or cheaper spiced wax. (See also *Pouncet box*.) From mid-16th century compartmented pomander box for perfumed powders **(333**: closed and open). Range of 17th-century shapes – book, skull and so on – reproduced by Victorians.

Pontil mark, pontil rod, also punty Thin iron pontil rod was used to hold base of blown glass vessel while shaped and finished. Attached by heat; removed by sharp stroke, leaving scar.

331 Poker work, stool, *c.* 1900

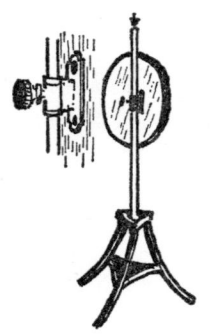

332 Pole screen, back view

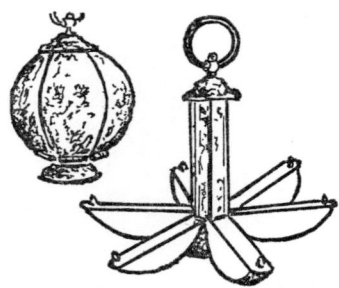

333 Pomander, closed and open

After *c.* 1750 this smoothed by grinding on good glass but found as late as mid-19th century on cheap work.

Pontypool (Monmouthshire) japanned ware From 17th century. Became important under William Allgood using tin-plated sheet-iron brilliantly coloured with hard-glazed, heat-resistant varnish. Trays from early 18th century (**334**: Victoria shape), soon followed by candlesticks, urns, tea kettles and so on. Glowing grounds of crimson, scarlet, yellow blue, 'tortoiseshell', brown, variously decorated. Also from near-by *Usk* (q.v.). Birmingham (Baskerville) from *c.* 1750; extensively in South Staffordshire from 1770.

Porcelain Translucent Oriental ware made by high-temperature firing of china stone and china clay. From 1740s England made frit or soft-paste porcelains – Chelsea, Bow and so on – but these were imitations. English hard porcelain first made at *Plymouth*. See also *Frit* and *Hard-paste porcelain*.

Portland or Berberini vase About 50 B.C. Vessel in *cameo glass* (q.v.) from Alexandria, once owned by Duchess of Portland. Familiar from Wedgwood's copy in jasper ware 1786–90 – 29 specimens in first edition and more subsequently (**335**).

Posset pot Silver specimens remain from late 17th century. Shallow, lidded, spouted two-handled vessel made also in slipware and English delft ware (**336**); pewter; glass. By later 18th-century vessel was lidded, two-handled 'caudle cup' of porcelain or creamware. Invalid's hot posset drink of spiced cream and wine was followed from 1720s by hot caudle containing egg and oatmeal, especially for young mothers and their visitors.

Posy holder From early 18th century but hand-carried mainly from 1820s through Victorian days. Shaped either as a tapering trumpet, a cup with stick or crook handle, a curving cornucopia or any of these modified to include tiny folding legs. Silver, metal filigree, machine-pressed gilt-metal (**337**); handles of porcelain, painted enamel, ivory, shell, amber, coral, glass. Often pin to hold posy; some more elaborate devices.

Pot lid Victorian. Slightly rounded lid of white-glazed earthenware with multi-colour pictorial decoration. Jesse Austin, 1806–79, working for potters F. & R. Pratt, Fenton, introduced in 1845 a method of transfer-printing pictures on lids (flat until *c.* 1848)

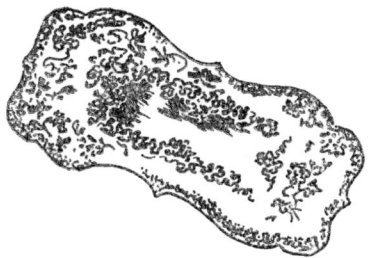

334 Pontypool tray – Victoria shape

335 Portland vase, jasper ware copy

336 Posset pot in tin enamelled ware

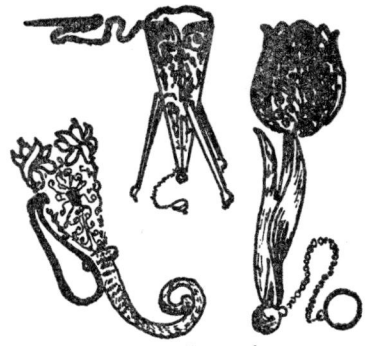

337 Posy holders, gilt-metal

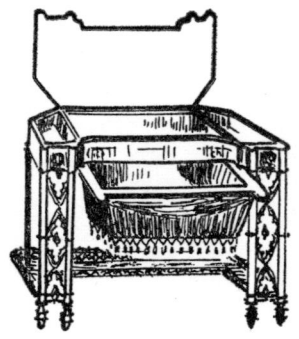

338 Pouch table, open (Sheraton design)

339 Pratt ware jug

340 Pressed glass

of pots used by makers of hair pomades and fish pastes. Some signed by Austin or, rarely, by T. Jackson. Many subjects reissued from original printing plates.

Pottery Ceramic wares other than porcelains. Claywares, often incorporating other ingredients such as sand, flint, baked in kiln, becoming earthenware or hard, vitrified stoneware according to degree of heat used for firing.

Pouch table From second half of 18th century. Work table distinguished by fabric pouch or bag hanging from frame below the working surface. This could be drawn forward for access to work too bulky for the drawers above. May have vertically sliding firescreen at back (**338**: Sheraton design).

Pounce pot Pot with perforated (pounced) lid, balancing inkpot on inkstand. Contained finely-ground gum-sandarac powder, often called sand. Mainly used to check flow of ink on absorbent unsized paper and to improve surface after erasures. In 19th century, with sized, unabsorbent writing paper, the vessel was, in fact, used for sand, sprinkled on slow-drying ink.

Pouncet box From mid-16th century. Successor to pomander but containing sponge soaked in herb-enriched aromatic vinegar. Sometimes mounted on top of cane. As sponge box, continued to late 18th century when more potent vinegar prompted development of tiny vinaigrette.

Powder blue Porcelain ornament with granular effect, noted, for example, on 18th-century Worcester. Dry powdered *smalt* blue (q.v.) blown down a tube through a filter of lawn on to oiled surface of ware before glazing.

Pratt ware About 1790–1830s. Cheap gay earthenware often with moulded relief ornament painted with enduring underglaze *high temperature colours* (q.v.), often with mottling. Jugs (**102, 339**), mugs and so on. Felix Pratt was a notable manufacturer but established as late as about 1803.

Pressed glass From 1830s. (**309**: Sowerby & Co.). Molten glass forced into surface-patterned mould with a plunger (**340**), such vessels being patterned outside in imitation of cutting but smooth inside and have no pontil marks. Cheaper than free-blown and wheel-cut glasses. Finish improved by *fire polishing* (q.v.).

Pricked pictures From *c.* 1770s. Simple pastime enjoyed by George III's daughters. Portrait engraving printed on period's normal rag-paper had details of dress elaborated into effects of slight relief (about $\frac{1}{16}$ in.) by pricking from back with needles in wooden handles in range of sizes. Outlines, folds and so on worked from front, then filled in from back. Exotic Oriental 'Turkish' figures popular, often hand-coloured and set against 'sober opaque colours' as recommended in *The Young Ladies' Book*, 1829. *Shadow pricking* arranged for viewing with light from behind. *Roulette pricking* with many-pointed wheel tool applied commercially to some valentines before introduction of embossing machine.

341 *Prie-dieu* chair

Prie-dieu Early Victorian single chair with long straight back, flat topped, and low seat (341). Could be used for family prayers but popular as setting for pictorial cross-stitch embroidery in Berlin wools.

Princes metal, or Prince Rupert's metal Invented 1670s. Costly form of burnished brass (5 parts copper, 1 part zinc), its tone much resembling gold, long used for good quality clock spandrels and so on.

Princess Charlotte 1796–1817. George IV's daughter whose brief life prompted many interesting souvenirs, whether celebrating her marriage to Prince Leopold in May 1816 (as on printed quilt centrepieces) or commemorating her death the following year. Portraits in ivory, ceramics (plaques, medallions), and crystal cameos.

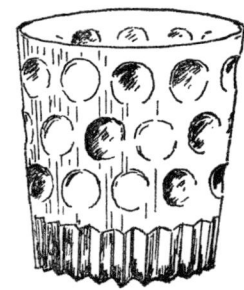

342 Printies on Regency glass

Printies From 1740s but more especially 1790s–1830s. Glass ornament. Groups of small circular hollows wheel-ground into surface of glass, lightly in fashionable thin glass of 18th century and more deeply into the toughened, gleaming glass of 1800s (342). As 'bull's eyes' appeared in profusion on pressed glass.

Prismatic cutting, step cutting 1790s–*c.* 1820 and again in 1830s, responding brilliantly to gas lighting. Simple, deeply cut parallel V-section grooves (342) achieving splendid refractive effects in the period's rich flint-glass.

Prisoner-of-war work Napoleonic wars meant over 60,000 held in this country, including many craftsmen permitted to make and sell small articles composed from available materials. Especially *bone* work (343), *straw-work* (q.v.) but also rolled paper *filigree*, crochet gloves, hair jewellery, artificial flowers.

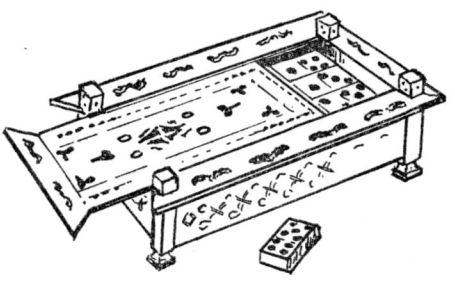

343 Prisoner-of-war work in bone

344   Prunts on early glass stem

345   Punch kettle and brazier (Wedgwood stoneware, engine-turned)

346   Two varieties of purled ornament

Prunts   Glass. From 17th century. Ornament on stem of early flint-glass drinking glass like small seals or bosses which, when tooled, are called strawberry or raspberry (**344**). Also on 19th-century fairings of trailed or streaked *Nailsea glass*.

'Published by' mark   Occasionally on early 19th-century ceramics such as elaborate jug designs by W. Ridgway & Co. (1835) and C. Meigh (1840). Shows design was entered at Stationers' Hall to secure 14 years' copyright protection.

Punch ladle   From late 17th century. Silver (**244**: changing shapes), Sheffield plate. Early cylindrical bowl followed by hemispherical and goose-egg shapes in 1720s and oval, often double-lipped in 1730s. Circular spoutless bowl frequent from 1740s, elaborated later. Shell-shape around 1750. Early handle silver, or turned ivory, ebony or other hardwood. Coin inset in bowl no help in dating. See also *Toddy ladle*.

Punch pot, punch kettle   18th–early 19th centuries. White or red stoneware (**345**: Wedgwood, engine-turned), porcelain and so on. For serving hot punch. May be mistaken for large teapot but lacks teapot's characteristic strainer inside base of spout.

Purled ornament   From 1670s on flint-glass hollow-ware. (1) Short outer case or layer around lower part of vessel, mould-shaped into ribs which were often swirled or waved in later 18th century. Effect comparable with silver gadrooning and obscured wine sediment (**346 left**). (2) Moulded all-over diaper of small round or oval compartments (**346 right**).

Purls   From 16th century. (1) On lace, tiny loops or picots as border ornament. (2) Metal thread lace. (3) More generally, tiny tubes formed of close-coiled silver-gilt wire like flexible beads for sewing among seed pearls and spangles on wear-resistant embroideries. Many remain in inferior silk-covered copper wire.

Puzzle fan   Form of *brisé fan* (q.v.) with a greater number of blades. Opening the fan reveals only half of each blade so that proper manipulation presents two alternative painted scenes on each side.

Puzzle jug   From 17th century; many 19th and 20th centuries. Slipware, English delft (**347**), stoneware, earthenware, bone china.

Vertical neck has pierced ornament so that
liquor in body of jug has to be obtained from
one of the several spouts projecting from a tube
linked with hollow handle. All but one spout
and perhaps also an inconspicuous hole have to
be covered before drinking.

347 Puzzle jug, tin enamelled ware

Pyramid 18th century. Glass. For the dessert. Two or three glass salvers in decreasing
sizes, placed on top of each other, each ringed
with individual glasses of sweetmeats and topped by large orange glass **(348)**. See also
Dessert glasses.

348 Pyramid of glasses for dessert

349   Quaiches of wood (*top*) and silver

350   Quail pattern (Bow)

351   Quartetto tables (Sheraton design)

Quaich   Scottish drinking cup, at first formed of wooden staves hooped together and with two lug handles **(349 top)**. From 17th century often in silver or pewter with flat handles ornamentally pierced **(349 bottom)**.

Quail pattern   Popular on English soft-paste porcelain (Chelsea, Bow **(350)**, Worcester): adaptation of Oriental Kakiemon pattern with two plump little quail or partridge birds in setting of rocks and foliage.

Quartetto tables   From late 18th century. Small occasional tables in graduated sizes to nest three or four together. For this reason all but smallest had three instead of four stretchers linking legs, sometimes of brass wire **(351:** Sheraton design). Like early version of *teapoy* (q.v.), could be used as individual tea tables.

Queen Anne   1702–14. Term widely misused by earlier collectors and writers who gave name to later revivals of period's features. Associated with arching cabinet furniture **(230)**, bended-back cabriole–leg chairs **(71, 165)** and a new pleasure in curved outlines **(170, 381)**, gracious proportions and plain, smooth surfaces in furniture, silver **(175, 406)**.

Queen's ware   Cream-coloured earthenware as improved by Josiah Wedgwood. Immensely popular tableware with strong, uncrazed yellow glaze. Name used by Wedgwood by permission of Queen Charlotte, wife of George III, from 1765.

Quill cleaner   Vessel weighted with small lead shot to steady it when its rim holes supported feather quill pens. Shot helped clean pen-nibs of clogging ink. Frequent component of inkstand; sometimes introduced as outer compartment around metal or china inkpot.

Quilting   Two layers of fabric, often with interlining, held together by lines of plain stitching, forming patterns in low relief **(352)**, many traditional. Worn under medieval armour, in Tudor, Stuart and Georgian dress and for timeless bed warmth and elegance.

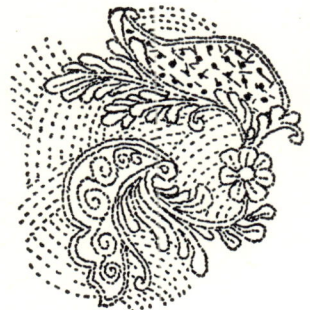

352 Quilting, pattern detail

Quintal vase From second-half 18th century. Ceramic flower holder with five sockets fanning out from substantial base. Catalogued by the Leeds firm in creamware (1783) as quintal flower horn (353).

Quizzing fan Second half 18th century. Perforated border covered with transparent material enabled user to be observant while feigning modesty. A late specimen might include a quizzing glass – spyglass – set in guard above rivet.

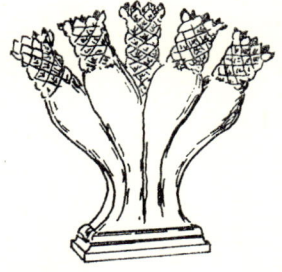

353 Quintal flower holder (Leeds)

Rail Furniture. Horizontal piece of constructional framework as in seat framing and above and below panel.

Raising Metal work. Flat sheet of silver or other metal shaped into hollow vessel by long hammering on a wood block, with frequent heating (annealing) to keep the work from becoming springy.

Rasp Mainly late 17th–early 18th centuries. To grate plug tobacco to make snuff, outmoded by commercial snuff-grinders. Perforated iron grater about 8 in. long, framed in silver, ivory, boxwood, often with hinged, sliding or pivoting cover. Spouted cavity under grater to collect powder for filling pocket snuff-box (354). See also *Nutmeg grater* and *Snuff mull*.

354 Rasp for snuff with pivoting cover

Ratafia glass Flint-glass from late 17th century, of small capacity for potent cordial (brandy infusion of fruits). From 1740 very narrow tapering flute glass, with drawn stem and plain foot twice diameter of bowl (355). Associated by collectors with ratafia but this distinctive design probably intended for much stronger brandy surfeit water.

Rathbone, Thomas From *c.* 1808 important Scottish potter at Portobello Pottery, Edinburgh. Popular wares (356) such as cheap bocage figures, wall plaques including pieces commemorating visits of William IV, 1822 and Victoria, 1842. Succeeded by son Samuel. Firm closed 1850.

355 Ratafia glass

Ravenscroft, George 1618–81. Extremely important in developing *flint-glass* (q.v.) 1674, improved 1675, long unrivalled in Europe for sturdy, resonant table glass of great refractive brilliance.

Red stoneware From 1684, used by John Dwight of Fulham (see *Fulham stoneware*). Hard fine-stoneware for teapots. Harder version with clear-cut ornament patented by S.

356 Rathbone earthenware fisherwoman

Bell, 1729. In early 1760s Wedgwood called his version rosso antico. Followed by Wood, Spode, Hollins and others. Highly polished, used under copper lustre in 1820s.

Reeding Furniture, metal work. Two or more parallel mouldings in convex profile introduced vertically in much neo-classic ornament (357). Opposite of fluting.

Refectory table Recent name for simplest version of long dining-table (358) as distinct from draw and trestle designs.

Regency period Strictly 1811–20 but applied by collectors to c. 1795–1825. Some delightfully simple design emphasised by rich furniture veneers, brass ornament; massive silver, gilded porcelain. Graeco-Roman shapes as well as ornament (75). Also Egyptian motifs (145) reflecting Napoleonic campaigns; escapist imitation of Oriental lacquer, bamboo; and occasional pinnacled neo-Gothic romanticism (359: leopard monopodium, long glass or psyche, typical reeded leg and lion paw; other illustrations of period include 120, 144, 188, 318, 409, 428, 454, 455, 519).

Registration marks 1842–83. Ceramics, metalwork and so on. Diamond-shaped mark with central *Rd* printed, impressed or incised to show design or decoration was protected from copying (80, 360). Symbols at diamond points can be interpreted to give details such as date registration was made at Patent Office (not date of marked object's manufacture).

Registration number From 1st Jan. 1884 straightforward numbering (from 1) replaced mark described above. By end of 1899 this had reached *reg. no. 351201*. Hence higher numbers indicate 20th-century manufacture.

Relief print From 14th century – as soon as suitable paper available. Opposite of intaglio print. Parts required to show white on page were removed from, e.g. wood block and remaining projections inked for paper to be pressed lightly upon them – no *plate marks* (q.v.). Important because could be printed with type-press. See also *Woodcut* and *Wood engraving*.

Renaissance Early 16th century, reaching England from Italy. 'Rebirth' of classical style and craft skills, loosely interpreted but distinct from Gothic, producing opulent, elaborate furniture ornament, silver and so on, much enjoyed and distorted by Victorians.

357   Reeding on late 18th-century chair

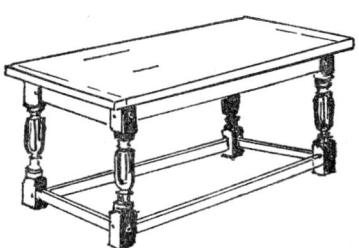

358   Refectory table, late Tudor

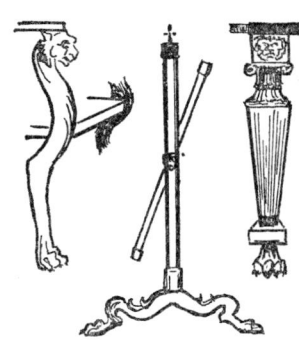

359   Regency lion furniture details (on chair, dressing glass, table leg)

360   Registration mark

361 Resist lustre ware

362–363 Restoration period: silver caster (1683) and Charles II walnut and cane chair

364 Ribband back chair, Chippendale design

365 Typical Ridgway pattern-title mark

Repairer, ceramic Misleading term for figure maker who put together separately mould-shaped parts of a figure before kiln firing.

Repoussé work See *Embossing*.

Resist lustre From *c.* 1810. Ceramic ornament. Resist applied overglaze temporarily protected pattern from metallic oxide solution painted over whole surface. When resist was washed away pattern appeared in silhouette against metallic lustre ground. Pattern usually white or cream until 1830; occasionally hand-painted yellow, pink, apricot, blue. Birds **(361)**, leaf patterns, formal flowers, fuchsias (from *c.* 1850), scenes, on jugs, goblets and so on.

Restoration period Years immediately following restoration of monarchy (Charles II), 1660 **(362, 363)**. His court brought back from Continent many new fashions in furniture, silver and other rich furnishings.

Ribband back Chair design introduced 1754 but not originated by Thomas Chippendale. Back splat elaborated into rippling curves suggesting intertwining ribbons **(364)**. Involved skilful carving and gluing of dense early mahogany.

Ridgway family From 1802 potters at Cauldon Place, Hanley. John died 1814, his sons trading as J. & W. Ridgway until 1830. Then John Ridgway & Co. to 1855 while W. Ridgway & Co. operated Bell Bank Pottery. Both important potteries making household and cabinet wares. Often small initials discernible in pattern-title marks **(365)**.

Rock crystal Hexagonal crystal, colourless or slightly bluish or yellowish. Long regarded as protection from poison, which would colour it. Fairly easily shaped as small vessels, panels for boxes, miniature and locket frames and so on until clear glass became commonplace.

Rockingham, Swinton, Yorks Pottery from 1745; J. & W. Brameld from 1778; in partnership with Leeds Pottery, 1787–1806. From 1813 directed by W. Brameld's three sons; from *c.* 1825 products included fine bone china richly decorated and gilded **(366)**, frequently now finely crazed. Griffin mark in red introduced 1826; puce mark from 1830 (e.g. in tea service saucers). Closed 1842 but J. W. Brameld continued decorating china cabinet wares in London to 1854 with *Brameld* mark.

Rockingham glaze wares From *c.* 1790 at Rockingham (Swinton) pottery of good quality earthenware; soon in general use at potteries making red earthenwares. A lead glaze heavily stained with oxide of manganese to a lustrous purple brown. As it ran during firing the lower parts of a vessel tend to be most deeply coloured. Late 19th century with wheel engraving and other ornament by Wedgwood. Wide Victorian manufacture for everyday wares at Sunderland, Middlesbrough, Alloa, Stirling, Swansea, Derbyshire and elsewhere.

366　Rockingham china teapot

Rococo style (104, 367, 451). 19th-century name for early Georgian adaptation of French *rocaille*. Light-hearted escape from heavy Baroque. Sophisticated pleasure in well-balanced disorder and fanciful ornament such as asymmetrical cartouches, opposing C-scrolls, shells, rocks, waterfalls, flowers, often intermingled with *chinoiserie* motifs (q.v.). Revived, heavy-handedly, from 1820s. Pre-Chippendale enthusiasts included B. & T. Langley (1740), M. Lock, H. Copland. Found in range of media from looking-glass frames to trade cards.

Rodney jug From 1782, Derby porcelain **(368).** Round-faced mask of Lord Rodney (1718–92) in admiral's cocked hat forming large spout to serving jug. Commemorated popular admiral's decisive victory over French (West Indies battle of the Saintes) two years after his victory over Spanish at Cape St. Vincent. Much copied; also mugs (Rodney decanter **394**).

367　Bracket in rococo style

Rolled gold Substitute for solid gold, cheaper even than much-alloyed 9 carat gold for 'toys', lockets and so on. Produced by fusing gold very thinly on to base metal such as copper. Better than electro-gilded gilt metal.

Rolling pins, glass Late 18th-early 19th centuries. Filled with salt – later sweets. Of cheap, dusky bottle glass at first tapering slightly to ends. Found in successive Nailsea styles: brownish green with coloured flecks; striped and mottled **(294)**; plain deep blue, amber, green with painted ornament; opaque white painted or transfer-printed with good-luck verses.

Rose engine turning See *Engine turning.*

Ruby glass Late 17th century, deep red; ruby tone patented 1755 (Mayer Oppenheim). Clear, heavily leaded flint-glass usually with gilding, now lost. Popular again from 1820s in range of metallic oxide reds, e.g. for *cased glass* (q.v.). More 'fancy glass' from 1870s for wide

368　Rodney jug, Derby porcelain

369 Ruby glass, Victorian

370 Rummer of 1800s

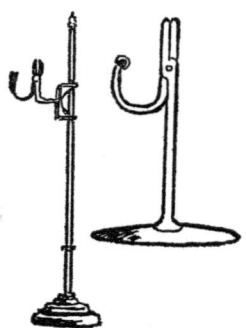

371 Rushlight holders, floor and table styles

market, cheaply blown or mould-shaped and loaded with frills and crimpings (369).

Rummer From 1750s, glass for long drinks such as rum and water. Goblet with ovoid bowl, short drawn stem, small foot. Fluting on bowl hand-cut from 1770s, blown-moulded from 1800s. Square foot from *c.* 1790. Larger rummer for hot toddy from late 1780s; bucket and barrel bowls from 1800s (370).

Rushlight holder 17th–19th centuries while (and after) candle tax restricted home production of cheap lighting. Law allowed use of common soft rush, peeled to leave one or two strengthening ribs and 'passed only once through grease or kitchen stuff and not at all through any tallow melted or refined'. Flimsy, so holder had to grip it near tip with scissor action nippers, one arm weighted to ensure grip. Holder could be moved up and down vertical iron rod with safety stop above wooden or iron base (371). Change from wrought iron to cast iron in late 18th century. Table, floor and hanging versions. Where available splits of pine wood preferred.

Rustic work Georgian delight in sophisticated rusticity reflected in mid-18th-century patterns for arbour and grotto furniture, shepherd porcelain figures, crabstock handles on useful wares. But much remaining is Victorian, such as gnarled, ivied branches for iron garden seats and tree-trunk chairs of ceramic ware with niches for mosses (372).

372 Rustic ceramic seat, Victorian

Saddle seat Especially associated with Windsor chairs used from early 18th century. Thick block of wood (essential for stuck-in legs and back) permitted surface shaping with slight depressions to sides of central low ridge. Sitter could lean back without sliding forward on uncushioned wood (**278, 373, 509, 510**).

Sadler & Green Liverpool. From *c.* 1756 early specialists in transfer-printed decoration, first on tiles. Later other ceramic wares. Potters, including Wedgwood, sent wares for this monochrome ornament in black, red, purple.

Sadware Flatware – plates, dishes, chargers – made of first-quality lead-free pewter ('tin-and-temper', basically tin toughened with a little bismuth and copper – later antimony). Mould-cast and lathe-rasped but given compact strength by laborious hammering (hammer marks showing on underside of the *bouge*, q.v.) by specialist sadwaremen.

Salamander Wrought iron. Round or square disc nearly inch thick, on long handle (**374**). Thrust into fire until red hot then held over pastry, cheese and so on, for quick surface browning. Early type had small legs to support disc in heart of primitive down-hearth fire.

Salopian China Manufactory See *Caughley*.

Salt, Ralph 1782–1846. Minor Hanley maker of earthenware figures in primitive manner of *John Walton* (q.v.), including rudimentary bocage backgrounds.

Salt-glaze For *stoneware* (q.v.) to give clean, hard surface. Common salt shovelled into specially designed furnace at moment of highest temperature so that sodium in salt combined with silica in ware to give it thin hard film of soda glass, non-poisonous, durable but with somewhat granular texture. Found

373 Saddle seat on Windsor chair

374 Salamander

375 Salt-glazed white stoneware, mould-shaped jug

376 Samplers, 17th (*left*) and 19th centuries

377 Sand burning: shell motif

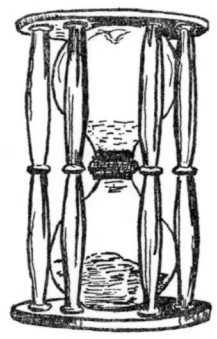

378 Sand glass, early Georgian

on white stoneware teapots, brown domestic and public house vessels (**375**: mould-shaped white salt-glazed stoneware jug).

Salver, glass Through 18th century. Flat plate with low vertical rim on pillar stem with wide foot. See also *Pyramid*.

Salver, silver About 1650s–1730s, small silver dish-shaped tray on pillar foot now known to collectors as tazza. From *c*. 1715 simplified version for minor servant duties had three or four small feet. Waiter, for similar carrying duties, was plain plate shape.

Sampler Mainly from 16th century onwards as miscellany of needlework stitches. 17th century, band sampler with rows of line stitches and white work on narrow linen strip, sometimes yard or more long (**376 left**). 18th century, more marking alphabets. Became child's show piece, rectangular, worked with improving verses, borders, pictorial motifs, on yellow linen or worsted tammy cloth (**376 right**). Some maps; some fine darning on tiffany. Early 19th century, dominated by *cross-stitch* (q.v.); often faked and of minor interest.

Samson porcelain From 1845 made by E. Samson et Cie of Paris, as deceptive reproductions including 18th-century English soft-paste porcelains, such as Chelsea; also Sèvres and many others.

Sand Confusing name for gum sandarac preparation used on unsized paper. See *Pounce pot*.

Sand burning From 17th century. Hot sand used to shade and mark wood for marquetry detail (**377**).

Sand glass Hour glass. Two flint-glass pear-shaped bulbs joined by narrow waist, held vertically in frame – wood, silver, ivory. Sand in one bulb falls into other in measured time when frame is inverted. From *c*. 1720 two glass units heat-welded together around brass bead (**378**). From *c*. 1760 glass blown as single unit with corked hole at one end for inserting sand or marble dust. Quality of glass aids dating.

Sand picture or marmortinto From *c*. 1780s, pulverised marble, dyed and glittering with mica, used as sugar substitute to make scenic backgrounds to porcelain figures on dessert tables. From *c*. 1790 pictures fixed to shallow trays or plateaux with nut oil varnish and sold by china sellers. From 1840s coloured sands instead of marble dust, such as found at Alum Bay, Isle of Wight. Originated by G. L. Haas, confectioner and Windsor Castle table-decker, followed by Benjamin Zobel, in London from 1784 and son James, b. 1791 (who made 'paintings' after Morland, occasionally signed), F. Schweickhardt, E. Dore and others.

Satin glass Victorian coloured and shaded fancy glass given peach-skin surface by immersion in hydrofluoric acid. Most valuable is *pearl-satin glass*, patented 1857 by Benjamin Richardson. Glass vessel shaped with indented pattern by blowing into mould, then cased in second layer of glass, forming air-pockets with quilted effect **(379)**. Late Victorian in shaded colours. Imitations European and American, at period and today.

379 Satin glass with 'quilted' ornament

Satinwood Popular 1760s–1800s, 1860s–80s. Golden tones with silky sheen **(431)**. West Indian more richly golden, with fine grain; East Indian paler with dark streaks. High-quality furniture, especially as veneers.

Scagliola Imported from Italy for English use, 17th century; English made from *c.* 1760 as substitute for costly marble. Plaster of Paris and glue suitably earth-coloured and enriched with small pieces of marble. Highly polished for table tops.

Scent bottles 18th–19th centuries. Porcelain **(417)**, bone china, fine-stonewares, glass **(79, 380)**, painted enamels and so on. Included figures and other imaginative shapes and such mid-Victorian novelties as the double-ended bottle in deep-cut coloured glass **(right)** or glass-lined silver, half containing flower 'handkerchief scent' and half smelling salts based on liquid ammonia.

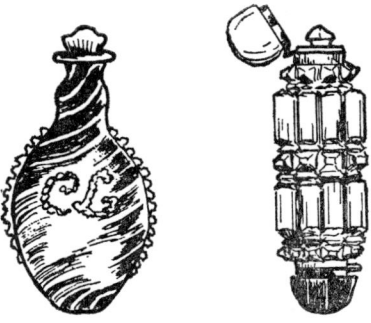

380 Scent bottles, 'Nailsea' glass (*left*) and double ended

Sconce From 16th century. Wall light composed of backplate and one or two branches bearing candle sockets **(381)**. Backplate in silver or brass elaborately embossed gave reflected light attractive sparkle but mostly ousted by mirror glass in early 18th century. Occasionally with framed embroidery illuminated by the candle.

Scottish snuff-boxes Laurencekirks or, after 1820, Holyroods. From *c.* 1790s, sycamore, often horn-lined, notable for hand-carved wooden hinge popularised by James Sandy. Cheap from 1830s. Some with painted copies of famous pictures. From *c.* 1870s followed general practice of printing the ornament, either on light wood or on paper pasted on. Early makers included Crawford of Cum-

381 Sconce, brass, 1700s

382 Scratch blue ornament on white stoneware

383 Scrimshaw work

384 Seal on bottle, dated 1722

nock, W. & A. Smith of Mauchline. Some tartan boxes. See also *Tartan ware*.

Scrapbook or album Mainly 19th century. Young lady's hobby. Original work increasingly augmented by professional items, e.g. professionally scissor-cut scraps, much advertised 1820s–30s (flower groups, sporting scenes, *Dr. Syntax* illustrations, q.v.) as sideline by profile cutters. Special steel engravings from 1840s; embossed glossy coloured lithographs from 1870s for composing page groups. Amateur talent in *Amelias* (q.v.), hair 'family trees', fern and seaweed ornament.

Scratch blue From *c.* 1720. Ceramic ornamented with incised line patterns in blue (**382**). Ware could be colour-dipped, then covered with white slip, scratched away to reveal underlying colour. Or powdered blue-stained glass could be dusted into incisions scratched in body before firing (frequent on white salt-glazed stoneware).

Screws in furniture From later 17th century brass screw pins in wide use in cabinet making; slotted heads but hand-filed irregular threads. Lathe-shaped from *c.* 1760; machine-made, gimlet-pointed from early Victorian days.

Scrimshaw work Mainly 19th century. Jack-knife carving and incised work picked out in paint or lamp black on whale bone and teeth, available to whaling ship sailors at sea (**383**). Especially stay-busks as love tokens but also snuff-boxes, bodkins, rolling pins and so on.

Seals, bottle From 17th century, vintner-filled bottles supplied by rich customer. Such bottles, with embossed seals bearing crest, coat of arms, cypher or name of owner, some dated (**384**: 1722), frequent to 1830s, customer supplying brass die to glass-man.

Seals for wax Precious metals, gem-stones, marble, hardened steel. More finely cut from late 17th century because better sealing wax. Glass from *c.* 1740, opaque white from 1770s, coloured especially after 1845. Fine stonewares from 1770s. Desk seals (carved handles); ring seals (some revolving bezels); pendant (cut with standardised motifs) all still popular with Victorians (**385**: one with revolving bezel).

385 Pendant seals (revolving bezel, *bottom left*)

Secretary, secretaire Late 18th-century name for chest of drawers or table (**386**: Shearer design) containing deep top drawer with fall front and desk fittings; sometimes cupboards below. Development of late 17th-century scrutoire cabinet with fall-front. Many late Victorian.

Seddon, George 1727–1801. Extremely successful London cabinet maker and upholsterer with flair for lavish display but shrewd interest in mass production, resulting in great quantities of simple mahogany and painted furniture.

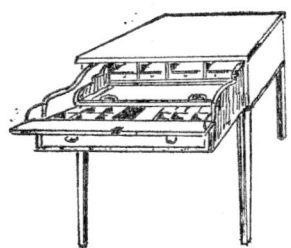

386 Writing table with secretary drawer (Shearer design)

Serpentine Furniture outline, mainly 1750s–80s with later imitations (**387**). Commodes, tables and so on with top outline carried through front and sides: central convex swell flanked by concavities, giving prominence to front corners often ornamented (carving, ormolu). Preceded plainer bow front.

Serpentine rock For ornaments, columns. Green, red, brown, often handsomely mottled. Softer than jade. Found in large masses at the Lizard, Cornwall. Traditionally poison-revealing, for drinking vessels.

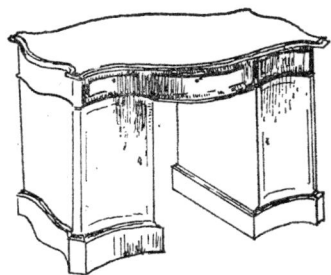

387 Serpentine furniture outline

Sgraffito ornament See *Incised ornament*.

Shagreen Hardwearing waterproof skin with granular surface for gluing on cases (fan, jewel, instrument), usually dyed green (**388**). (1) 17th–18th centuries, of asses' skin; (2) of other animals' skins, artificially roughened. (3) 18th century onwards, of shark-skin, then named nurse-skin (from dogfish) and fish-skin (from ray fish) with spines filed smooth.

Sham-dram Spirit glass of deceptively small capacity for tavern keepers' use. Small, sturdy, with heavy stem and foot; often folded foot in early manner on 19th-century vessel.

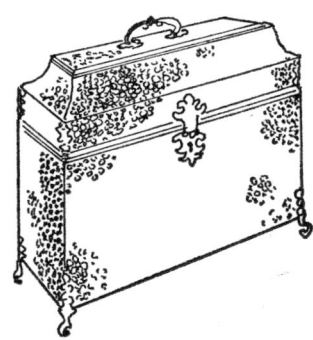

388 Shagreen tea chest

Sham drawers Mainly later 18th-early 19th centuries (**188, 390, 430**). Handles and mouldings to suggest drawers on front or side of chest furniture, either to mask a desk-well or cupboard or to balance a set of real drawers on other side of piece such as davenport.

Shawl Wide traditional use but especially 1800s–70s, prompted by dress styles (**389**: border detail 'Indian pine' pattern). Superb Kashmir, imitated Norwich from 1784. See *Paisley* below. Some silk and cotton. Printed (Paisley and elsewhere) from *c.* 1850s with sewn-on fringes, reversible from *c.* 1860 (same

389 Shawl, border detail of 'Indian pine' pattern

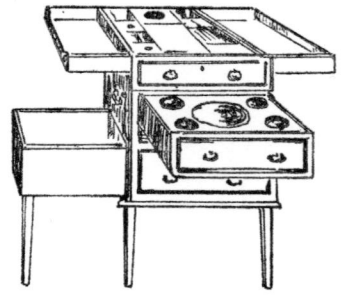

390 Shearer design for dressing stand (priced at £2 6s.)

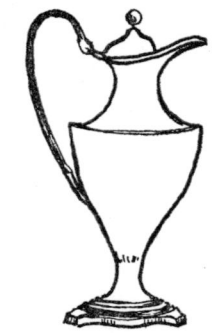

391 Sheffield plate neo-classic design

392 Shell work: posy and two details of heart-shaped box

pattern both sides in reversed colours). Lace, often copied cheaply in tambour stitch on machine-made net. See also *Nottingham lace* and *Pillow lace*.

Shawl, Paisley From end of 18th century. With ornamental borders from *c.* 1805; more decorative from 1815; made by Jacquard loom from late 1830s in Kashmir patterns, some in 'cashmere' wool from English-reared Tibetan goats. Name Paisley applied only to shawls with woven pattern.

Shearer, T. 18th-century furniture designer and cabinet maker. Illustrated in trade catalogue *Cabinet-Maker's London Book of Prices* (1788 and later editions) and in *Designs for Household Furniture*, 1788 **(386, 390)**. None of his own furniture can be identified.

Sheffield plate English invention of Thomas Bolsover, 1742. Table ware and so on in style of solid silver but much cheaper **(153, 391, 455, 495, 511)**. Ingots of silver and copper fused under heat were rolled until as thin as silver plate and similarly hand-raised, soldered, chased, pierced, die-shaped, drawn for wirework **(516)** and so on. Until 1760s silvered on one side only: interior or underside might be tinned. When silvered on both sides manufacturer still had to mask red copper edges: see also *Mounts on Sheffield plate*. Marks mainly after 1836. By then rivalled by *British plate* (q.v.).

Shell work From 17th century but what remains mostly Victorian. Amateur hobby: small shells glued to caskets, toilet mirror frames, 'temples, vases, flower pots' as advertised 1755. Costly decoration for elaborate country-house grottoes, such as by *Mrs. Delany* (q.v.) who also made shell flowers but deplored indiscriminate colouring such as 'yellow and purple oysters'. Late Georgian and Victorian delight in tall groups of shell flowers under glass domes **(392 top)**; boxes covered with tiny iridescent shells (rice work) until became cheap commercial work **(392 bottom**: heart shape cardboard box with shells and pincushion).

Sheraton, Thomas 1751–1806. Came to London *c.* 1790 where worked as author, publisher, not making furniture. So-called Sheraton furniture follows designs or styles he drew and described in his *Cabinet Maker and Upholsterers' Drawing Book* (four parts), 1791–4 **(123)**; *Cabinet Dictionary*, 1803 and *Encyclopaedia*, first volume 1805 **(75)**. Light, somewhat effeminate treatment of neo-classic style with emphasis on straight, vertical lines, careful attention to such details as feet, metal inlay, ingenious devices (Other designs **323, 338, 351**).

Sherratt, Obadiah 1776–1840s, succeeded by widow Martha and son. Burslem, Staffs. From *c.* 1810 made earthenware figures such as ambitious chimney ornaments on distinctive footed bases. These included groups of robust figures illustrating story-telling themes, topical, religious, humorous (**393**: 'Ale Bench').

393   Sherratt figure group 'Ale bench'

Ships' glass   Designed to minimise hazards of rough weather. Decanter (so-called Rodney from 1782): heavy, with expansive base, straight sides tapering quickly in uninterrupted line to base of neck (**394**). Drinking glass: short stumpy, with thick, spreading foot sometimes half as wide again as bowl-rim. May be confused with *firing glass* (q.v.).

Silesian stem   20th-century term for glass with shouldered pedestal stem first used for silver candlesticks *c.* 1700 and popular for drinking glasses to *c.* 1790. At first four- or six-sided, sometimes pinched into vertical reedings (**395**). Eight-sided from *c.* 1740s. Sometimes inverted or double (head to head).

Silhouettes   Especially *c.* 1780–1850, mostly anonymous. Methods have no chronological sequence and include: painting on ivory, card, sometimes highlighted with gold or bronze; painting on back of clear glass, backed with gold leaf or tinsel; painting inside convex glass against flat white plaster (shadow effects); inside glass in outline surrounded by black and backed with colour; black profile (painted) with coloured uniform or dress; cutting from paper, or silk, with knife, later scissors.

394   Ship's glass decanter

395   Silesian stem on drinking glass

135

396 Silicon ware, carved (Doulton, *c.* 1882)

397 Silver lustred earthenware

398 Singing bird box, Victorian

Silicon ware From 1880. One of Doulton & Co's art wares. Vitrified brown stoneware, smear-glazed. Decoration, before firing, included carved **(396)**, incised, perforated work, applied mouldings, pâte-sur-pâte slip, colours such as blue, brown, green, grey, with traces of gilding, copper lustre.

Silvered glass 1848 Drayton patent for sealing a silvering solution between two layers of glass. London firm, J. Powell & Sons, associated with this work. Cheaper than mercury process used for mirror glass. Vases, inkstands, goblets. Some shallowly cut or ground (frosted). Sometimes coloured transparent glass over the silvering for luminous effects, by E. Varnish and others.

Silver-gilt Silverware covered with thin film of gold, often as protection from tarnish or stains of acid, egg and so on.

Silver grain Attractive greyish lustre displayed in oakwood when planks from quartered log are taken along radiating medullary rays of its natural growth.

Silver lustre From early 1800s. Ceramic wares silvered, by use of platinum oxide, either all over **(397)** to suggest silver plate (mainly after 1823), or in patterns (see *Resist lustre*). White glaze linings and surface painting from *c.* 1845. Cheaper – poor – from 1852.

Silver, sterling From Middle Ages, standard of quality required of English silversmiths (assayed – tested – by their guild) except 1697–1720 (see *Britannia standard*). Pure silver (925 parts) alloyed with copper (75 parts). See also *Hallmark* and *Lion marks on silver*.

Singing bird box From *c.* 1770 as tiny exquisite watchmaker-goldsmith-jeweller creation in shallow box, cane-head, bracelet. Bird's song achieved with minute spring-impelled bellows forcing air through tube whistles. Further mechanism to make bird movements. Early birds enamelled, later feathered. Cheaper from 1860s, in boxes like vinaigrettes **(398)**. Elaborate cages of singing birds by automaton-maker James Cox, London, from 1760. Caged birds mounted on musical boxes mainly from 1830s on. Cages, gilded brass, japanned iron, wood, often Birmingham-made to house Continental birds and mechanisms.

Skewers 18th–19th centuries. Silver and imitations, *c.* 6 to 15 in. long, made in sets for dining-room use to aid host carving at table.

At first resembled age-old wooden skewer (often lignum vitae from 1680s). From *c.* 1750s tapering bodkin shape, flat, with hole at top (changing from long slit through oval with ornament to round by 1765). Spoon pattern ends from *c.* 1770 and arrow shapes.

Skillet Cast bronze, sometimes cast brass. Early saucepan, like small cauldron: used to side of open down-hearth fire, so had long straight handle **(399)**. In silver used on charcoal brazier.

399 Skillet of bronze

Slate Ancient material revived 19th century, mainly 1820–60s. Tough, non-absorbent, cheaper and lighter than marble for table tops and so on. Painted by japanning process to resemble marble or with flowers and so on in manner of contemporary marble inlay and papier mâché, the colours hardened by prolonged heat.

Slide, slider (1) From 18th century. In cabinet furniture, a flat, rimless tray pulled out like drawer to serve as table **(49, 444)**. Small ones for candlesticks, sometimes dished, on furniture for reading or toilet use. (2) For decanter: see *Wine coaster*.

Slip Potters' clay watered down, usually to consistency of cream. Clays turning different colours when kiln-fired could provide range of tones from cream and buff to reds and browns.

Slipware Ancient, primitive, but much made in 19th century. Coarse earthenware covered or decorated with slip after shaping and galena-glazed **(469)**. Slips trickled **(479)** or dotted on ware from spouted pots; or intermingled in marbled or combed effects **(506)**; or as all-over coating (see also *Incised ornament*) or filled into surface hollows on mould-shaped ware. Overcame early problem of colours running under lead glaze. Occasionally more solid pads or lines of clay pressed into surface of ware **(400**: sophisticated use, late 19th-century Barum ware, Barnstable).

400 Slipware (Barum ware, Barnstable, 1880s)

Smalt Refined preparation from cobalt oxide (discovered Saxony 1545). Used by potters as they developed wares white enough for blue ornament. Was one of few colours that could be protected by application underglaze. See *High temperature colours*.

Smear glaze From later 1830s. Ceramic glaze applied as vapour or mist in glazing kiln. Used on domestic parian ware **(401)** such as

401 Smear glazed parian ware bowl

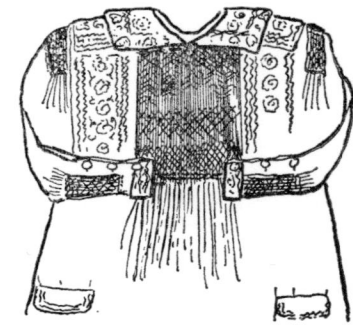

402 Smock

403 Smoker's bow chair, Victorian

404 Snuff-box in painted enamels, *c.* 1770s

elaborately moulded jugs **(312)** and vases, the fine granular surface being given very slight gloss, difficult to keep clean. Often used on exterior of vessel which was lead-glazed within.

Smelling bottle Term long used for *scent bottle* (q.v.) but to mid-Victorian it replaced *vinaigrette* (q.v.), containing revivifying scent based on liquid ammonia sweetened with attars of rosemary, lavender, bergamot and cloves. Often of thick glass, deeply cut or harnessed with silver to protect contents from heat and evaporation. Silver cap covered inner glass stopper **(380)**.

Smithum Mainly pre–1750s when outmoded by liquid lead glaze, but long continued on primitive-style slipware. Lead ore in powder form scattered on earthenware; kiln firing produced clear glaze tending to rich iron-yellow tone.

Smock, smock-frock Most elaborate early 19th century, using ancient name **(402)**. Functional loose over-garment of linen or cotton drill used by drover, shepherd, woodman and other all-weather workers. 'Pillow-case-cut' made comfortable and strong by stitched gathering front and back and on upper sleeves and cuffs. Traditional colours and regional patterns in supplementary embroidery (feather, stem, herringbone stitches) on collar, shoulders, front panels. Genteel for ladies around 1880s.

Smoker's bow chair Victorian, farmhouse, tavern, smoking-room variant of heavy 'Lancashire windsor'. Massive armrests forming continuous horizontal bow supported by turned spindles and only a little deeper at back, with shaping to fit sitter **(403)**. Padded leather variant named Eaton Hall chair from 1867.

Snuff-bottle Late 17th–early 18th centuries. Cylindrical, of glass made opaque-white with tin oxide, its stopper ground to ensure tight fit, with ball finial. Imitation of exquisite bottles carried by Chinese.

Snuff-box From late 17th century. Gold, silver, pewter, brass, painted enamels **(404)**, tortoiseshell, ivory, hardstones, papier mâché, horn, turned and carved wood. Flattish pocket size and larger for table use. Some double boxes. Tight-fitting lid, usually hinged. Increasing demand for cheaper boxes from 1760s. Ornament ranged from individually commissioned painted miniature and costly jewels to engine turning or transfer-print.

See also *Scottish snuff-box* (Illustrations include **247, 448**).

Snuffers From medieval days. In wide demand, often elegant, until 1840s when wick improvement obviated need. Silver, Sheffield plate, steel, including cut-steel, brass, iron. Scissors shape, one blade fitted with box, to trim, quench and retain charred wick or snuff, so that candle burned brightly **(405)**. From 1749 occasional mechanical devices: dates known if patented.

Snuffers stand From *c.* 1690s but less used than tray. Silver **(406)**, brass. Socket on stem and broad foot with loop handle at side, to hold snuffers vertically, handles upward for easy access. Sometimes including candle socket opposite handle.

405 Snuffers and snuffers on tray, 17th century

Snuffers tray From 1660s. Silver, Sheffield plate, japanned iron, Victorian papier mâché and so on. To hold snuffers laid flat and also hot snuff cut from candle. Dish-shape followed by shallow tray. At first outline of snuffers or rectangle **(405)**. Early Georgian waisted oblong often with handle and with low rim because by then snuffers might have three small feet for easy lifting. Late 18th century some elliptical; *c.* 1800 four-lobed, to include cone extinguishers. Florid from *c.* 1820.

Snuff handkerchief From late 17th century. Especially 19th century to 1870s. Some silk, mostly cotton. Some picture-printed: topical, political, instructive. Copper plate printed monochrome outlines from 1750s, on smoother calico from 1774, black, purple, light brown. In red from *c.* 1800, then blue and green; stippled shadows from *c.* 1815. Great increase from early 1830s. Bandanna introduced by 1792 by James Bayley.

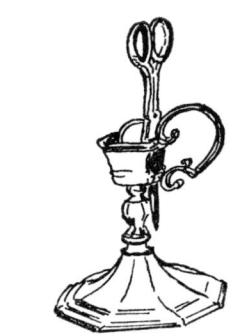

406 Snuffers stand

Snuff mull From late 16th century, introduced to London from Scotland. Ram's horn, exterior polished and interior cut with sharp ridges: thus user could grind own snuff from plug of tobacco. Wide end fitted with hinged cap – silver, ivory, horn or bone. Large mulls for table use **(216)**.

Snuff rasp See *Rasp*.

Soapbox From 1660s through 18th century. Silver, brass **(407)**, turned wood, painted enamels. For soapball or wig powder. Small near-spherical vessel on wide foot, the upper half opening as lid, often hinged, and usually ornamentally perforated. Alternatively base

407 Soapbox

408 Sociable, Victorian

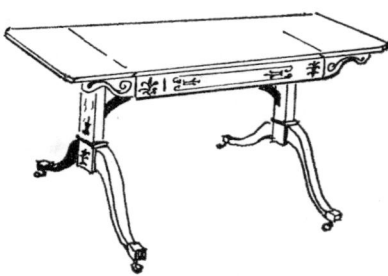

409 Sofa table

410 Souvenir horse brass (Victoria jubilee)

411 Spider table, *c.* 1770s

perforations might release moisture and soap's perfume. See *wash-basin stand*.

Soapstone porcelain From late 1740s. Soft-paste or frit porcelain containing 35–45 per cent finely pulverised steatite from Cornwall. Dense, heavy, hard-textured; important because resistant to temperature changes including use with boiling water. Associated especially with useful wares of Worcester, 1751–1820s; also with early Bristol, some Liverpool, Caughley.

Sociable Mainly early to mid-Victorian. Upholstered seat for two people side by side, composed of two conjoined armchairs either half-facing each other or facing opposite ways **(408).**

Sofa table From late 1790s. Long narrow table usually with trestle-type end supports on to out-jutting castor-mounted feet **(409).** Top extended by small end-flaps. Often fitted for games and with drawers and sham-drawers in frieze. For two people sitting on sofa or settee.

Soft-ground etching Popular late 18th century. Printed from acid-cut, ink-filled hollows in copper plate, like usual hard-ground etching. But acid resist (of softer wax) on the copper plate was covered with paper and etcher drew in pencil so that removal of paper removed corresponding lines of wax. Acid 'bit' these soft-edged lines into the copper plate. Result somewhat resembles roulette-cut 'crayon etching'.

Soft-paste porcelain From early 1740s. Included nearly all 18th-century English porcelain – Bow, Chelsea, Derby and so on – introducing glassy *frit* (q.v.) to achieve translucence. Oven-fired twice – before and after glazing – but at much lower temperature (about 1100° F.) than the single-firing of hard-paste porcelain. Lacked cold appearance of hard porcelain and could be marked with file.

Souvenirs for collectors Can concentrate on subject (coronations, political events); personalities (18th–19th-century royalty, celebrities); or type of article used for commemorative work (printed fans, horse brasses (**410**: with crude piercing for Victoria's jubilee) and especially such earthenware as mugs, wall plates, loving cups, jugs and Victorian mantelshelf figures).

Spandrel Triangular space between outer curve of arch and right angle formed of mouldings enclosing it: hence corner ornaments on clock face beyond dial perimeter.

Spider table Mainly third quarter 18th century when was the only fashionable gateleg table. With six or eight legs, including four fixed and one or two for each of the two gatelegs swinging out to support falling flaps. All extremely slender turned spindles left square for each point of junction with equally slender stretchers (**411**).

Spiers & Son, Oxford 19th century. Showed at 1851 Exhibition. Specialists in papier mâché ornament. City views and so on, including commissioned work, painted on trays, tables, screens, cabinets, workboxes which they bought as blanks or already gilded from Alsager & Neville of Birmingham. Sometimes inscribed with their name.

Spindles Furniture. Lathe-turned rods, plain or showing decorative variations in thickness which may aid dating. Cheap alternatives to carving for chair back, table leg, as on windsor chair (**19, 189, 403, 509**). Split lengthways, were glued to front of cupboard furniture as ornament in 17th century.

Spinet From 17th century, name for wing-shaped development of much earlier rectangular virginal, with similar keyboard and plectrum action to create vibrant string music.

Spinning wheel From about 14th century. Treadle-operated wheel turned horizontal spindle twisting thread as spinner drew it from carefully prepared mass of wool, flax or cotton. From 17th century, wheel might also turn faster-revolving bobbin to wind the spun thread at required tension, regulated by flyer. Vertical supports for spindle, bobbin and flyer known as the sisters, mounted on T-shaped movable base – the mother-of-all (**412**).

Spirit flask Especially 1820s – late 1840s for shelf display in taverns. Brown and buff salt-glazed stoneware by Bourne of Denby, Doulton (**413 left**: 'Mr. and Mrs. Caudle'), Vauxhall, Oldfield, Green of Lambeth and others. At first flask shape with cameo celebrity portrait. Soon head and shoulders in full relief formed upper part of flask, often with political slogan below. Imitative shapes from clocks to pigs and powder horns.

Spit Ancient method of roasting meat in front of open fire. Wrought-iron bar, with sliding fork prongs or meat-holding basket, rested on spit-dogs (andirons with hooks for

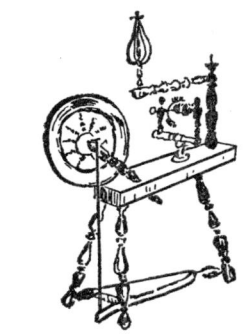

412 Spinning wheel

413 Spirit flasks: *on left* Mr and Mrs Caudle (Doulton)

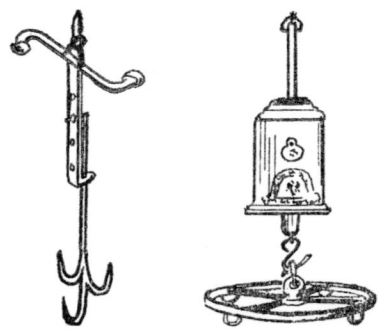

414 Spit jacks: dangle spit (*left*) and bottle jack

415 Spode: saucer pattern no. 2387 (1804)

the purpose) to sides of fire. Early spit turned by servant or by dog in rotating drum attached by chains and pulley.

Spitalfields silk   Refugee weavers from Flanders, established 1580s; augmented by Huguenots after Revocation of Edict of Nantes, 1685. Guild of silk weavers founded 1629. Successful until early 19th-century development of power looms.

Spit jack   For mechanical spit turning. From late 16th century with weights and gears. Later spring-driven clockwork. Smoke jack, 18th to early 19th centuries, had rotor in chimney driven by hot air from fire. Weighted dangle-spit turned on cord **(414 left)**, at its neatest in late bottle-jack **(right)** hanging over fireplace or in Dutch oven.

Spit rack   Pair of cob irons, each with hooks on a vertical bar to support spits while cooling and out of use.

Splat   Furniture. In chair back, the central vertical piece between the cresting rail and either a lower cross-rail or the shoe-piece on back seat-rail. Important from late 17th century; curved to fit sitter's back (bended back) early 18th century (Illustrations include **165, 278**).

Spode, Josiah   1733–97; also son and grandson (d. 1829) of same name. From 1770 own earthenware factory, Stoke-upon-Trent. Developed underglaze *transfer-printed* ornament (q.v.). Firm evolved spectacularly successful bone china from 1794; feldspar porcelain from *c.* 1800; stone china from 1805; parian wares from 1842. Firm continued by W. T. Copeland (Copeland & Garrett 1833–47) and direct successors, many marks incorporating name Spode **(415**: saucer pattern number 2387, 1804; **453**: teapot).

416
Spoons, Hanoverian, knop and rat-tail (*right*); also handles in Onslow, puritan, slipped-in-the-stalk, cat's head and trifid patterns

Spoons Silver, some gilded, pewter, Britannia metal, brass, plated metals, horn, wood. (Illustrated **416**, in order of mention.) *Hanoverian pattern c.* 1715–30s, with tapering central ridge running short way down front of stem from rounded, upcurved tip of handle, comparable with 'rat tail' on bowl. *Knop pattern*, mainly pre-1660s with solid casting – acorn, lion, apostle, seal – soldered to end of straight stem, with fig-shaped bowl. *Onslow*, towards mid-18th century, with wide scroll top to waisted stem at period when S-curve was changing to smooth arch and bowl from ellipse to egg-shape. *Puritan*, mid-17th century, straight stem cut off without ornament, contemporaneous with slanting cut at top known as *slipped-in-the-stalk*, soon elaborated slightly into *cat's head* and similar flattened, notched and three-pointed (*trifid*) ends. *Rat tail*, mainly 1670s–1720s, with line of stem continued down back of bowl as tapering rib. See also *Fiddle-back silver*.

Sprigging Clear, undercut relief ornament on jugs, mugs, teapots, shaped separately in small moulds and immediately applied – sprigged – to body of ware before firing (e.g. **82, 426**). Easily distinguished from inferior mould-shaping of whole relief-ornamented vessel.

Sprimont, Nicholas (1716–71). Trained as silversmith at Liège. Came to England 1742 and entered name at Goldsmiths' Hall. Now mainly associated with Chelsea porcelain factory, being its dominant personality from 1746 (**417**: goat-and-bee jug, scent bottle).

Springs Patent 1828 by Samuel Pratt for spiral coiled wire springs in mattresses and seats. Fixed to canvas or interlaced webbing, sewn into box shapes and further strengthened with cane or whalebone. But long-continued demand for earlier style of padding with curled horsehair.

Spun glass From late 17th century for cheap ornaments. See also *Friggers*. Used by Benjamin Richardson, Stevenson & Williams and others for Victorian ornament, closely-wound on epergnes and the like (**418**), using threads spun by hand on revolving wheels; machine patented by Richardson mid–1860s.

Spun metal wares Mainly from early 19th century. Silver, Sheffield plate (**419**), brass, copper, Britannia metal. Method of shaping hollowware, cheaper in time and material than earlier hand raising. Flat disc of rolled metal

417 Sprimont, Chelsea, goat-and-bee jug and scent bottle

418 Spun glass thread ornament on glass, 1860

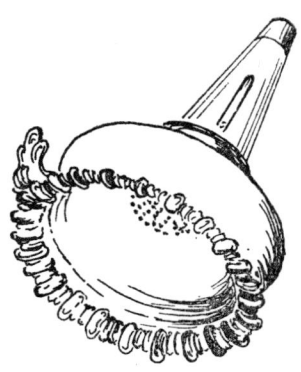

419 Spun metal (Sheffield plate) wine funnel, early 19th century

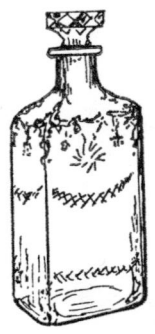

420 Square with gilded ornament

placed against wooden block or chuck revolving in lathe, forced against it by tool of steel or hardwood until acquired hollow shape.

Squab From 17th century. Cushion to fit chair seat (523) which had low rim to hold it.

Squares Glass decanters intended especially for close packing in chests for travellers. Design mainly high-shouldered, with short neck. Many blown-moulded from *c.* 1745 onwards; some expensively free-blown. Spirit squares often locked in handsome cases. Pint and half-pint sizes for cordials, toilet waters; some gilded (420), some ornamentally cut (aid to dating).

Stamped metal From *c.* 1770s. Drop hammer and fly press increasingly used for shaping and ornamenting silver, Sheffield plate (421), brass, Britannia metal, and so on. Cheap because quick and required thin metal. Improved results when harder steel generally available for tools from *c.* 1790s. Sections of vessels stamped and assembled, if necessary weighted with lead-tin fillings. Die-stamping could produce ornament embossed or perforated.

421 Stamped metal (Sheffield plate) Regency teapot

Standish and inkstand From 15th-century tray holding writing equipment which developed into compartmented inkstand. Silver, Sheffield plate, pewter, often with glass vessels, ceramics. Developed into elaborate set with harmonising vessels for ink and pounce, shot-weighted quill holder and cleaner, sealing wax taper-stick, wafer box, pen tray (290). In 19th century *pounce pot* (q.v.) and wafer box adapted for sand and postage stamps.

Statuary porcelain See *Parian ware.*

Staunton chess set Design by Hon. Howard Staunton, son of Earl of Carlisle, registered at Patent Office 1849. Exclusively English, made by John Jacques & Sons, London, in boxwood, natural colour and dyed red or black. Conventionalised shapes (422).

Steel engraving From *c.* 1820. Intaglio print taken from engraved steel instead of copper, the steel softer than engraver's tool. Very many more impressions could be taken before the metal plate showed signs of wear. From 1840s engraver could cut into copper and take a few high quality prints before the plate was steel-surfaced for the main run of prints.

422 Staunton chess pieces – queen, bishop, king

Sterling See *Silver.*

Stevengraph From late 1870s. Name given by Thomas Stevens to his most elaborate style of picture ribbon, 6 in. × 2 in. with mount of stiff gilt-edged card bearing printed title, to sell at one shilling; framed, half a crown. Mail coach and railway scenes, historical and sporting occasions, (**423**: boat race), celebrity portraits. Brilliant use of colour and extraordinarily fine background detail creating three-dimensional effects entirely by loom weaving. See also *Picture ribbons*.

423 Stevengraph on typical lettered mount

Stick barometer From 1660s and continued in manufacture to 1840s. Wall barometer for home use. English invention. Changes in atmospheric pressure measured by movements of mercury up and down vertical tube rising from small cistern, all handsomely framed. First half 18th century often cornice and broken or arched pediment (**424**). Later oval face and oval patera covering cistern.

Stiles Furniture. In panelled work, the vertical members into which rails are tenoned to form framework around panels. Intermediate verticals are muntins.

424 Stick barometer, early Georgian

Stipple engraving Mainly from 1760s. Etching (acid) process but usually worked over with graving tool. Achieved delicate, effeminate effects with great numbers of dots or flecks instead of lines, their spacing determining intensity of shadow. Frequently found printed in shades of red and brown or in combinations of red and blue tints. Many reproductions of portraits (Gainsborough, Reynolds and so on). F. Bartolozzi best-known exponent (in London from 1764).

Stirrup cup From *c.* 1750 in silver; *c.* 1770 in earthenware (**425**). Also noted in porcelain (Chelsea-Derby, Derby), fine-stoneware, bone china. Drinking vessel to be emptied at single draught. Shaped as animal's head – fox, hare, terrier, hound; sometimes trout or clenched fist.

425 Stirrup cups, earthenware, hound head and fox head

Stone china From 1805, improved 1810. Developed by Josiah Spode II. Earthenware containing china stone. Hard, fine texture, ringing tone but opaque. Also made by Davenport, Wedgwood and others. Much mediocre work merely marked STONE CHINA.

Stoneware, brown From about mid-17th century (Fulham) when considerable imports from Continent such as *bellarmines* (q.v.). Plastic clay mixed with sand or crushed flint, fired at high temperature to become extremely

426 Brown stoneware Doulton tobacco jar with sprigged ornament

427 White stoneware, mould-shaped teapot

428 Regency silver by Paul Storr

429 Stourbridge engraved ruby glass

430 Straw-work cabinet

hard, opaque, heat resistant, entirely non-porous. Usually *salt-glazed* for strong, clean working surface; ornament incised, moulded or sprigged (**426**: tobacco jar). Colour depended on choice of clay. Jugs, *spirit flasks* (q.v.), mugs and so on. Much Victorian craft work (**274**), especially by *Doulton* firm (q.v.).

Stoneware, white salt-glazed About 1670s by John Dwight of Fulham (see *Fulham stoneware*). Refinement of above as substitute for Oriental porcelain. Fired at much higher temperature than comparable earthenware, making it hard, non-porous, somewhat translucent but brittle. Inelastic, so was mould-shaped or cast in sharp relief rather than thrown (**375, 427**): this and slightly granular 'orange skin' surface limited its table use to such items as ornate teapots, pickle plates and the like. Blue ornament (see also *Scratch blue*) 1740s; full colour enamel painting from 1750s.

Storr, Paul At work 1792–1821. Silversmith responsible for much massive Regency table silver (**428**). Ornate and heavy but controlled, well-proportioned design. Highly prized today and considerably copied.

Stourbridge glass From 17th century important region for glass making. Responsible for improved annealing methods; open-and-shut moulds; the first English pressed glass. Coloured glass from before 1750; much Victorian *cased* and *enamelled glass* (q.v.); glass threading machine. (**429**: engraved ruby glass). Museum (The Council House) has notable collection of coloured glass.

Strainer spoon See *Mote skimmer*.

Strapwork ornament From late 16th century. Popular with Victorians. Furniture, metal work, embroidery. Originally engraver's ornament, suggesting the up-curled edges of cut-outs in parchment or paper. Bands and borders of low-relief scrolls, interlacings, arabesques, around shields and lozenges.

Straw-work From late 17th century, recorded by Dr. Plot 1677, noting dyed rye straws cut into squares 'none larger than the 20th or 30th part of an inch' and glued upon wood or other hard surface to form views of buildings and the like. Amateur hobby; also much early 19th-century commercial work on boxes (**430**: toilet cabinet), tea caddies and so on, made and sold by French prisoners in England during Napoleonic wars. See also *Prisoner-of-war work*.

Stretchers Furniture. Horizontal rails linking legs of chairs, stools, tables. Elizabethan, low and plain, as foot rests (**236, 358, 363, 443, 509, 510**). Late 17th century became decorative. 18th century gradually outmoded in fashionable furniture, especially when made of mahogany, but retained in much of lesser quality or cheaper woods.

Strike-light pistol 18th century. Neat combination of steel, flint, tinder and sulphur match required to create flame before friction matches. Resembled flint-lock pistol. Flint triggered to strike steel so that fragments fell into tinder in pistol pan, making it smoulder sufficiently to light slip of wood, suphur dipped; these matches or spunks sometimes stored in pistol barrel (**432**: with attached candlestick).

Stringing Furniture. In veneer, very narrow square-section lines separating areas and borders; also lines showing checker effects in dark and light wood, sometimes suggesting rope-twist, popular from late 18th century (**431**: writing-paper box). Regency stringing often in brass.

Stuck-shank glass Drinking vessel with stem fused under heat to base of bowl (e.g. **457**). See *Drawn stem.*

Stumpwork Especially third quarter 17th century. Victorian name for raised embroidery mounted as pictures or on small furniture such as mirror frames, jewel cabinets (**433**), boxes. Mainly Old Testament figure scenes and limited range of heraldic and other animals, fruits and so on from popular published patterns, worked in fascinating range of stitches augmented with seed pearls, spangles, purls and applied to white satin. Some motifs padded; some partly detached to appear in relief.

Sucket glass 18th century. Stemmed vessel included among the individual glasses arranged on each tier of the dessert pyramid. For dry sweetmeats lifted with fingers, so tall-stemmed shallow bowl (wider than foot). Not used for drinking so often with ornamental rim such as open loops (**126 left**) or 'dog tooth' undulations (**434**).

Sugar tongs Silver (**435**). Scissor shape noted from 1708 onwards. Stork design around 1770s–80s and early Victorian. Simple bow shape with springy U-shape arch linking the stems probably in use from 1720s. Pierced stems in later 18th century; many plain with fiddle ends, matching teaspoons from *c.* 1805. Bigger to suit bone china tea ware from 1820s.

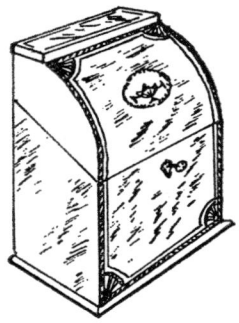

431 Stringing on satinwood desk box

432 Strike-light, with candle socket

433 'Stumpwork' cabinet

434 Sucket glass

147

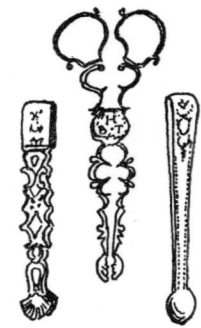

435 Sugar tongs, silver

436 Summerly's Art Manufactures: glass design by R. Redgrave, *c.* 1847

437 Sunderland jug with view of bridge

438 One-piece framed text in Sunderland lustre

Summerly's Art Manufactures 1846–50. Felix Summerly (sometimes identified by monogram FS) was pseudonym of Sir Henry Cole who became first director of South Kensington Museum. Attempted to improve standards of inexpensive factory-made goods by commissioning artists' designs, publicised by Felix Summerly's Home Treasury Office. Products ranged from parian ware figures and moulded jugs to ivory paper knives and some of earliest commercial Christmas cards (**311, 436**: papier mâché supper tray and painted glass water carafe, both designed by R. Redgrave).

Sunderland, Co. Durham From *c.* 1740 domestic earthenwares; from *c.* 1780 cream-ware; more conspicuous wares early to mid-19th century. Frog mugs, figures of lions and other chimney ornaments, jugs up to 2½ gallons, gift china. Recognisable ornament includes views of Wearmouth bridge, opened 1796 (**437**), portraits of Jack Crawford, local hero of Camperdown battle 1797, many verses and scenes for seafarers. Wide range of lustres – copper, pink, silver.

Sunderland lustre So-called though also made in Staffordshire, Liverpool, Bristol. From early 19th century. Splashed or mottled effects in purplish gold lustre (mixed gold and tin oxides) on 'framed' wall plaques (**438**), frog mugs and so on. Effect achieved with oil spattered on to the overglaze lustre: kiln firing produced bubbles which burst in irregular blotches.

Sunset glow glass See *Lime-soda-potash glass.*

Surface print From 1790s. Print taken from flat surface. Depended on chemical reactions (antipathy of water and oil) instead of the physical surface-cuts of intaglio and cameo or relief printing plates to retain or reject printer's ink as required for making print. Term especially for *lithographs* (q.v.).

Sutherland table Named after Harriet, Duchess of Sutherland, d. 1868. Small gate-leg table with trestle-type end supports to the narrow, space-saving central table-top compensated by very deep flaps (439).

Swan-neck pediment Especially early Georgian. Surmounting cornice on classic-style bookcase (440), wall looking-glass and the like, and long continued on long-case clock. Pair of opposing S-scrolls, their upper ends usually carved or brass-mounted with paterae and space between them for escutcheon, vase or other ornament.

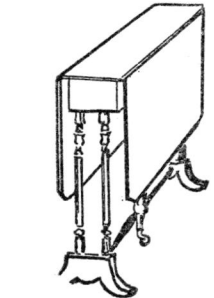

439 Sunderland table

Swansea porcelain 1814–17, at Cambrian Pottery, made by brilliant but erratic *William Billingsley* (q.v.). Soft-paste porcelain of varying formulae including *duck-egg porcelain* (q.v.), biscuit ware (441) and soapstone porcelain. (Mark, 270).

Swansea wares Several potteries. 1760–1870, Cambrian Pottery (see above): included fine quality earthenwares from 1790, bone china from *c.* 1820, imitation Etruscan ware (red terracotta with black figure ornament) from *c.* 1845, black basaltes, 1845–52. Glamorgan Pottery Works 1815–39: included many cow milk jugs, painted and transfer-printed. Landore Pottery, 1848–56.

440 Swan-neck pediment

Swash turning Especially 1670s–90s. Furniture (363, 442). Eccentric turning often known as barley-sugar twist on chair and table legs and hood pillars of long-case clocks. Copied from Dutch but less tightly twisted. Popular with Victorians who used pairs of opposing twists for symmetry (1).

Sycamore Valuable species of maple or false-plane, the wood white when young, yellowing with age. Close grain, often attractively rippled, non-warping, taking good polish. Considerable use for veneers, including stained, known as *harewood* (q.v.) or silverwood.

441 Swansea porcelain, white biscuit ware

Syllabub glass From *c.* 1720s. Included among individual sweetmeat *dessert glasses* (q.v.). For Georgian (whipped) syllabub, bowl in double-ogee shape, wide at top to make most of frothy whipped cream laid over base of sweetened sack or claret in narrow part below (126, 346, 348). With baluster, silesian twist or other decorative stem on domed or plain foot. Sometimes stemless, with knop between bowl and foot, omitted in 19th century.

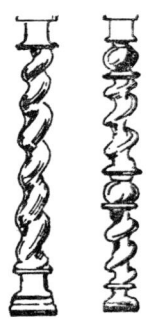

442 Swash turning

443 Tabouret

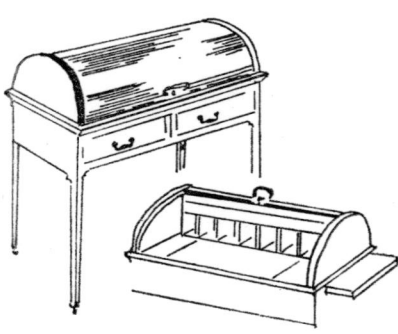

444 Tambour desk, closed and open

445 Tankard, 18th-century tulip shape

Tabouret   Defined 1656 as a low stool at a time when Continental tabouret etiquette permitted only certain women of high rank to be seated in monarch's presence: fostered by Charles II in England but subsequently observed only at court and only to 1760. Stool **(443)** with round, upholstered top – drum shape – still very popular with Victorians.

Talbert, B. J.   1838–81. Dundee woodcarver who became architect; designs included simple practical furniture in Gothic manner. London from 1865.

Tallboy   From *c.* 1690s. Double-height chest of drawers, often in two parts, the lower one fractionally larger with stepped moulding at join. Often deep cavetto cornice, canted front corners and heavy bracket feet. Evolved from chest of drawers on stand of late 17th century with drawer in stand-apron, also sometimes called tallboy.

Tambour   Furniture. Mainly late 18th century and Regency. Approved by Shearer and Hepplewhite (1788). Desk lid or small cupboard door rendered flexible to slide between straight or curved grooves. Composed of a row of narrow convex mouldings, their flat faces glued to strong canvas. Resembled carved ornament known as reeding and such a desk often known as a reed-top **(444)**.

Tambour frame   Most popular late 18th century. Circular embroidery frame composed of two hoops fitting inside each other with the fabric stretched between like drum-head. Often mounted on stand so that worker's left hand guided continuous thread or silk from the tambour spool while right hand held hooked tambour needle. Hence type of looped chain-stitch embroidery of eastern origin, amateur and professional, quickly worked with hook on muslin or other fabric in such a frame.

Tambour lace Early 19th-century embroidery worked with tambour hook on machine-made net as cheap commercial substitute for hand lace.

Tankard Medieval vessel of hooped wooden staves developing into Elizabethan cylindrical drinking vessel in silver or pewter with heavy handle and hinged lid raised by decorative thumbpiece (**143, 235, 445**: tulip shape). Many Victorian including design with glass bottom.

446 Tantalus with perfume bottles

Tantalus From mid–19th century. Stand or frame containing three squares – spirit decanters or perfume bottles (**446**) – apparently accessible but, in fact, secured by grooved bar or collar which had to be raised to release stoppers. From mythical king of Phrygia punished by tantalising sight of inaccessible water and fruit.

Taperstick From late 17th century, silver (**447**) and brass; later also Sheffield plate. Small versions of contemporaneous candlestick designs. For smokers, plain, without loose nozzle and largely ousted by friction matches in 1830s. For sealing, might be part of inkstand equipment (**290**). For teatime use from 1740s burning fragrant beeswax tapers, decorative designs including demi-figures fashionable mid-18th and early 19th centuries.

Tapestry Many medieval references. Fabric for hangings, upholstery, with pictorial, floral or other ornament created in course of hand weaving. Coloured pattern introduced in weft threads on framed warp of flax or hemp. English work much influenced by craftsmen from Continent. Barchester, Warwickshire, (William Sheldon) from c. 1560; Mortlake from c. 1619; Lambeth, 1660; subsequently Clerkenwell, Soho, Fulham and others.

447 Taperstick, early 18th century

Tappit hen See *Mutchkin*.

Tartan ware Especially from 1822 and through Victoria's reign (**448**). Snuff-boxes (See *Scottish*) followed from c. 1850 by wide range of minor wooden wares – cigar cases, workboxes, card trays, bellows. Hand-painted ornament of machine-ruled clan tartans (c. 100 varieties) often around celebrity portrait or scene. Inferior mass production from 1870s. Occasionally labelled, including Davidson, Wilson & Amphlet of Mauchline, Charles Stivens & Sons, Laurencekirk, W. & A. Smith, Mauchline.

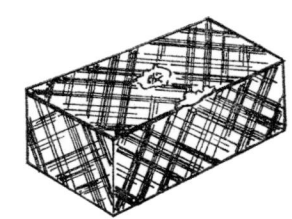

448 Tartan ware box

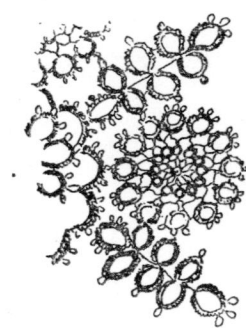

449 Tatting, detail

450 Tea caddies, wood (pear shape), and silver (1720)

451 Tea chest, serpentine outline

452 Barge teapot, Church Gresley

Tassie medallions Made by James Tassie (1735–99) and nephew William (retired 1840), famous for portraits in wax, who employed numerous modellers. Medallions were cast from wax in plaster and from plaster copies further moulds made for casting the medallions in very soft opaque-white lead glass. They lack undercutting of comparable work in jasper ware. Small cast for ring or seal, priced at 1s. 6d. in catalogue 1775.

Tatting From late 18th century, more popular from 1850s. Thread trimming to use like lace, composed of double knots built into loop patterns often with decorative picots (**449**), using a three-inch shuttle, sometimes two (tortoiseshell, ivory) and hairpin-type hook. Successor to large-shuttle *knotting* (q.v.).

Teaboard 18th-century name for lathe-turned tea-tray.

Tea-caddy, canister From 1680s; mainly through 18th, 19th centuries. Silver, Sheffield plate, ceramics, wood and other materials which could be fashioned into neat tightly-lidded box for dry tea (**95, 450**). At tea-table hostess or maid spooned leaves from canister to teapot or blended leaves from pair of matching canisters in glass bowl. Term caddy introduced c. 1770. Often two canisters and wider-mouthed sugar box formed matching set in tea-chest (**40**). Larger from 1780s. From 1790s term caddy applied to tea-chest.

Tea-chest From beginning of 18th century. Wooden box, lined with metal foil and often partitioned, for storing dry tea-leaves. Tea-trunks (covered morocco leather or shagreen with locks and silver mounts) for use at table (**388**) followed by flat-topped chests by 1750, velvet-lined to contain wooden tea boxes or metal canisters; some painted enamels (**40**). Popular through mid and later 18th century in contemporaneous furniture styles (**451**). See also *Teapoy*.

Tea-jar Porcelain: lidded vase for dry tea-leaves. By c. 1770 made *en suite* with tea-service by Worcester (**518**) and others.

Teapot, barge 19th century. Earthenware. Massive ornate design suiting brilliant painted decoration associated with canal narrow boats. Included late 19th-century Church Gresley (Leics.) design with miniature teapot as lid finial (**452**).

Teapot, Cadogan From c. 1790 in pearlware; from c. 1800 with dark brown Rockingham glaze. Some of 1830 onwards apple-green. Puzzle vessel with spout and handle but no lid opening (**453**: Spode). To fill, vessel inverted and strained tea poured into hole in base, where it passed down spiralling tube inside pot. First made at Rockingham, copying Oriental wine-pot lent by Hon. Mrs. Cadogan.

453   Cadogan teapot, Spode

Teapot, double spouted   About 1840s–80s. Cups filled from spout in normal position set low in body of pot. Secondary spout near top of pot facilitated preliminary pouring away of floating dust then expected in tea-leaves. See also *Mote skimmer.*

Teapoy, Georgian   Small light table for individual use when taking tea, most often pillar-and-claw design, its slender projecting legs often strengthened underneath with metal plate (**325**). From late 18th-century hostess might have her tea-caddy (chest) on similar table.

Teapoy, Regency   From *c.* 1810 caddy and table as single unit (**454**) composed of pillar stand supporting box which contained tea-canisters and often also bowls for blending tea-leaves and for sugar lumps.

Tea-urn   From 1760s through Victorian days. Silver and silver substitutes, copper, stoneware. Neo-classic shape. Developed from tea-kettle with tap (**455**: Sheffield plate, *c.* 1800). Kept hot with charcoal brazier (early) or box iron (patented 1774) or spirit lamp (cheaper fuels from 1830s).

Tea-urn, ceramic   From 1850 in heat-resistant vitreous stoneware, made, for example, by T. J. & J. Mayer (**456**). Elaborate designs with such details as demi-figure handles and sphinx feet.

Tea-urn, copper   Mainly after 1820. Many large, for inns, supplying hot water for coffee and toddy. Include tall Victorian vase shape with white china handles.

454   Teapoy, Regency style (*compare with no.* 325)

455   Tea urn, Sheffield plate, *c.* 1800

456   Tea urn, ceramic, T. J. & J. Mayer, 1851

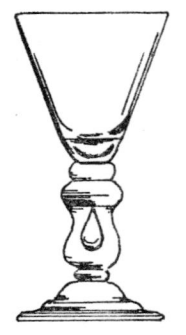

457 Tear in knopped heavy baluster glass, *c.* 1690s

458 Terracotta, Watcombe

459 Thimbles: on needlecase with seal foot (*left*), of Stuart brass (*top*), enamel (*centre*) and silver

Tear, glass Air bubble, enclosed in solid glass, as ornament (**239, 457**). Especially *c.* 1715–60, clusters in finials, knops.

Tent stitch Embroidery (**115**). See *Petit-point*. Tent or tenter (tenter-hooks) used to stretch fabric, hence a type of embroidery that required a stretching frame.

Terracotta Mainly Victorian. Soft form of earthenware, unglazed and porous with a slightly glossy surface suitable for painted ornament. Colour of fired clay ranged from rich red (sprayed with ferric chloride solution before firing) to yellow and brown. Much used for vases, conservatory ware, with painted Etruscan ornament. Makers included: Lowesby, Leics.; F. & R. Pratt (including clock cases); M. H. Blanchard (see *T. Battam*); W. & T. Wills (two-colour, hand carved to suggest lacquer); Coalbrookdale; W. Baddeley; Watcombe Terra Cotta Co., Torquay (**458**); G. Skey and C. Canning, Tamworth.

Tester From 16th century described canopy over bed, basically of wood with carved frieze supported by bed's head-board and two pillars at bed-foot. It thus formed ceiling over bedstock, being hung with curtains and often elaborated with embroidered draperies. Probably originally this was known as the bed's celour and the tester was what is now known as the tester (celure, selour) – the back of the bed-head, behind the pillows, made of fabric (embroidered with owner's arms) until introduction of Tudor panelling. See also *Angel bed* and *Four-poster*.

Thimble Used by Romans in bronze; medieval and much later included stitched leather; from mid-16th century gold, silver, silver-gilt, sometimes with motto on rim of separately made lower section. By 18th century included filigree work; hardstone caps; jewelled rims; painted enamels; early 19th century silver stamped with popular views; bone china. Also ivory, jade, bone, mother of pearl, wood. Workaday specimens, from *c.* 1600 mainly brass and/or steel, short and thick with hand-punched indentations. Followed by cast brass through 18th century and stamped from 1790s (**459**: silver with needlecase; Stuart brass; Georgian enamel; George IV silver).

Threading Silverware border ornament composed of simple engraved line, or two parallel, outlining, e.g. spoon-stem (**166**).

Throwing Primitive way of making furniture, ceramics. Shaping by use of wood turner's lathe or potter's wheel.

Thumb-piece Lever, purchase, billet. Silver (**460**: 1660s), pewter and other metals. On flagon and tankard, vertical or slanting projection above hinge of lid which fits on top curve of vessel's handle: thumb pressure holds lid open for pouring or drinking. Simple shape such as hammer-head, love-birds beak to beak, fleur-de-lys, scroll (volute, corkscrew and others), perforated designs (**143, 175, 235, 252, 445**).

460　Thumbpiece on silver tankard, 1667

Tin-enamelled earthenware Tin-glaze ware, English delft. Briefly 1560s (Flemish introduction). Mainly early 17th to late 18th

461　Tin-enamelled tiles, *c.* 1750s

centuries, aided by Dutch immigrants. Earthenware shaped, dried, surface-trimmed, fired to biscuit then dipped in lead glaze opacified with tin oxide (costly), producing dry white powdery surface for painting (no corrections possible), then kiln-fired. For extra gloss sometimes fired again after powdering with lead glaze in Dutch manner. Occasionally surface stained blue. Important because was earliest white ceramic surface suitable for ornament imitating Chinese porcelain. Blue and polychrome painting in *high temperature colours* (q.v.). Included Southwark from 1620s, Lambeth from 1660s, Brislington from *c.* 1640s, Bristol from 1680s, Liverpool, South Staffordshire (**44, 62; 461**: tiles, *c.* 1750s).

Tinsel picture Mainly 1820s–70s. Framed pictures, mostly theatrical figures, against painted backgrounds. Hobby developed from 'dressing' fashion plates and celebrity prints with pasted-on fabric scraps. Enthusiasm for theatre produced prints of actors, actresses: clothing cut away, replaced from behind with shaded fabrics and further ornamented with swords, shields, buttons and so on (**462**). These were supplied, e.g. by J. Webb, London, die-punched out of metal foil and sold paper-backed in range of sizes and prices from ¾d. Reproductions.

462　Tinsel picture, *c.* 1830s

463 Tithe pig group, Derby, *c.* 1765

464 Toasting glass

465-466-467 Three typical Toby jugs: Squire design by R. Wood (*top*), Martha Gunn (*centre*) and Whieldon colour-glaze style

Tint in flint-glass Colour tinge due to imperfect cleaning of ingredients. Black tint of lead oxide reduced from late 1690s. Iron's yellowish tint cleared by adding manganese. Suggestion of blue tint due to Derbyshire-mined lead found in much English and Irish flint-glass until 1810: occasionally to 1815 and in later imitations of 'Waterford blue'.

Tin ware Especially 16th to mid-19th centuries. Silvery white tableware frequently mentioned in early inventories. Makers were subject to Pewterers' Guild jurisdiction but by 1800 London had more workers in tin than in pewter. Teapots, lamps, ewers, tumblers and so on, often marked ENGLISH BLOCK TIN.

Tithe pig group Ceramics. From 1770s and through 19th century. Particularly popular figure group showing tithe-collecting cleric refusing to accept baby from harassed farmer's wife along with the tithe piglet **(463)**. Found as group by *Derby* (including Sampson Hancock), by Lakin & Poole and others; also occasionally as separate figures.

Toasting glass Late 17th-early 18th centuries **(464)**. Flute glass with slender stem about $\frac{1}{8}$th in. diameter to be snapped between finger and thumb after toasting a celebrity who might be named on the bowl, engraved with diamond ring. More substantial from around mid-18th century.

Toastmaster glass From *c.* 1740. Deceptive glass for long-established custom which required a sober toastmaster to announce and drink to long succession of toasts. Fine quality glass with straight-sided bowl – mostly solid glass – tall stem, solid conical foot. Sometimes found as presentation glass inscribed for important occasion.

Tobacco box From late 17th century. Round, rectangular or elliptical box with hinged lid. Distinctive because contained inner lid, weighted, to press upon tobacco and retain its moisture.

Tobacco jar Ceramics. Cylindrical with domed lid, sometimes with candle socket. Popular in brown stoneware with hunting scenes sprigged on **(426)**. Many Victorian.

Toby Fillpot Nickname for Henry Elwes, recorded in mezzotint print after Robert Dighton, with verses below, issued after his death, 1761, and also later by Carrington Bowles. Copied as sprigged-on motif in high relief for stoneware serving jugs, tobacco jars

(426), 1760s–1840s. Transfer-printed on earthenware with accompanying verse from engraving by R. Abbey (d. 1801).

Toby jug Figure of above modelled as jug for serving strong ale, not for common alehouse use. Unsmiling, lank-haired corpulent old man seated with jug and beaker; in long coat, breeches, buckled shoes (later tied), his three-cornered hat serving as spout. Earliest attributed to Ralph Wood, 1716–72, with ugly features suggesting modeller John Voyez. Many variants (Squire **465**: Wood), Nightwatchman, Martha Gunn **(466)** and so on) in range of colour techniques from early colour glaze **(467)** to Victorian Rockingham glaze and brown salt-glaze ware. Vast numbers of reproductions from 1890s on.

Toddy ladle From 1760s. Silver, Sheffield plate. Adaptations of *punch ladle* (q.v.) for newly-popular hot rum drink which affected wooden handle. Soon whalebone handle with twist-turned grip and silver ferrule. Hand-raised from flat silver in lipped designs by master silversmiths, often incorporating coins of earlier date. Lightweight factory-made ladles fluted or pattern-embossed.

468   Glass toddy lifter

Toddy lifter Glass, especially North England and Scotland **(468)**. For serving hot toddy from toddy rummer (massive version of toddy drinking goblet). Hollow tube with bulbous swelling and ribs for safe grip. Worked on pipette principle. Held between first and second fingers, plunged into liquor until full, lifted with thumb over upper hole to create vacuum so that moving of thumb released liquor into drinking glass.

Toft, Thomas Potters, father and son (d. 1689, 1703). Associated with many massive wall plates or chargers in slipware bearing their name. Ornament includes crude royalty and cavalier figures (several of Charles in oak tree) **(469)**; royal coat of arms, crowned lions and other heraldic motifs, Adam and Eve, and so on, frequently in criss-cross trellis borders.

469   Thomas Toft wall plate (Charles in oak tree)

Tôle peinte Collectors' name for fire-resistant articles of tin-plated sheet-iron with colourful japanned ornament. See also *Japanning, metal*.

Tompion, Thomas 1639–1713. Important English court clockmaker. Superb craftsmanship in weight-driven and spring-driven clocks, in well-proportioned cases; also watches. From early 1680s numbered his clocks, 1 to 542. Name on bottom edge of clock dial, at first in

470   Tortoiseshell and pearl shell card case

471   Tortoiseshell ware (fox and squirrel)

472   Typical touch marks on pewter

full in script writing; later, with abbreviation *Tho,* in printed lettering. Uncle of *George Graham* (q.v.).

Tortoiseshell   Popular from 17th century. Best was mottled outer shell of hawksbill sea turtle. Untarnishable, flavour-free and, under heat, could be shaped in relief and welded into large sheets, some as thin as $\frac{1}{16}$th inch. Used as veneer, often over coloured foil and for bijouterie such as fans, snuff-boxes, card cases (**470**: with mother of pearl). Ornament includes tooled embossing, *piqué* (q.v.) and posé d'or, *boule marquetry* (q.v.) and incised work.

Tortoiseshell ware   Mainly from *c.* 1750 onwards when Thomas Whieldon improved manufacturing methods often to be known as Whieldon ware (**471**), although widely made in the Potteries, Leeds, Liverpool. Earthenware coloured with metallic oxides that flowed and mingled in irregular markings when covered with transparent lead glaze.

Touch   Mark stamped on pewter indicating maker; sometimes quality. Makers' marks recorded on touch plate (sheet of pewter) kept by Pewterers' Company (**472**). Some resembled silver hallmarks. Inclusion of date indicated when pewterer introduced it, not date of article. Marks more usual on Continental pewter.

Toys   Ancient term for any amusing trifle, plaything or diminutive article. Through 18th century especially small elegancies for adults, widely advertised by specialist toymen.

Trade mark   Included in manufacturers' marks. Especially on ceramics. Used only from 1862 onwards (Trade Mark Act) and introduced still later by many firms. Hence aid in dating.

Trailed ornament   Glassware: decoration in relief with threads and ribbons of glass, clear or coloured, in wavy patterns, applied under heat (**52, 294 right**). Ceramics: lines and dots in semi-liquid clay slip trickled from quill or spouted pot on to coarse earthenware before kiln firing (**479**).

Transfer-printing   Battersea enamels, 1753 –6; thereafter Bow, Worcester porcelain; Sadler & Green of Liverpool (especially tiles); other ceramics to present day. Ornament printed on special paper from etched copper plate (some lithography from 1839) and thus conveyed to surface of ware before or after glazing. Underglaze from 1760s, improved by Spode

1780s (**473**: Spode 'Castle' pattern). Especially blue (**83, 508, 517**). Other colours underglaze from 1828; multicolour underglaze from 1848. See also *Pot lids*.

Transfer-printing on glass From *c.* 1760 onwards. Noted on enamel glass made at Perrins glasshouse, Warrington, such as vases. Black printing, sometimes over-painted in enamel colours.

Trays Fashionable mainly from 18th century. Wood (including marquetry), silver and other metals, japanned iron, papier mâché. Round, rectangular, elliptical, scalloped, pie-crust-rimmed. In wood had cabinet maker's built-up rim in contrast to plainer turned 'tea-board'. Collectable *picture trays* (q.v.) from late 18th century. Ceramic trays in *cabaret sets* (q.v.). See also *Butler's tray; Snuffers tray; Voider*.

Treen Small articles made of wood such as spoons, including collectors' Welsh *love-spoons*, (q.v.), *trenchers*, stay-busks.

Trencher From Medieval days; in use through 18th century. Wood, pewter, tinned copper. Primitive style of plate, *c.* 5 in. across, thin, more or less flat to facilitate use with knife: diners might cut their meat on trenchers before transferring it to more easily scratched plates of silver or glazed ceramic ware. Round, or square with corner hollow for salt. Some, 16th–17th centuries, painted with 'roundel' verses (**474**).

Tric-trac board From *c.* mid-18th century used for revival of early form of the game backgammon. Played on board surrounded by low gallery as noted in most late 18th-century games tables (**188**). Name from clicking sound of play.

Trifle Good quality pewter as recognised by Pewterers' Company. Of medium hardness, used for tough domestic wares such as drinking vessels and by triflers for the minor buckles and buttons and the trifles long known as toys. Collectors try to avoid old pewter re-cast, or acid cleaned (showing pitted surface).

Trivet From 15th century in wrought iron. Hollow ring on three legs to support cauldron over simple down-hearth fire, often with sideways projecting handle. Or with latten platform for supporting saucepan in front of fire (**475 bottom**). Variant hooked on to top bar of grate (**top**). See also *Footman*.

473   Typical transfer-printed plate: Spode, Castle pattern

474   Trencher, painted wood

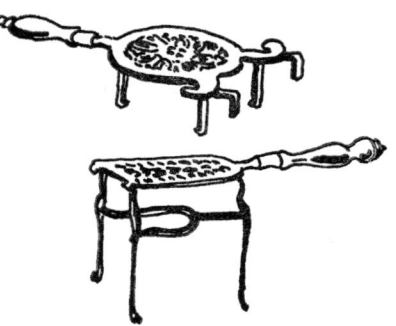

475   Trivets

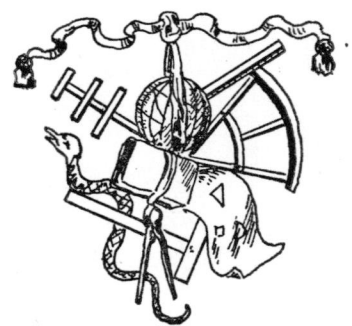

476 Trophy (drawing instruments from Chippendale bookcase design)

477-478 Tunbridge ware boxes in cube pattern and pictorial mosaic, with mosaic flower detail and 'stickwork' napkin ring

479 Tyg, slipware with trailed ornament

Trompe l'oeil ornament On furniture and so on, painted ornament such as groups of small everyday objects with naturalistic shadows and other detail to 'deceive the eye' into accepting them as real.

Trophy Ornament for carving, inlay, paint, composed from group of associated articles such as musical instruments or trophies of war (**476**: drawing instruments on Chippendale bookcase design).

Truckle bed, trundle bed From Medieval days. Low bedstock (with castor wheels from 18th century) pushed under standing bed during day and often used there at night also – for servant or child – as important beds stood high to discourage mice.

Tunbridge ware Mainly 19th century (**326**). Form of marquetry using mainly native woods in natural colours. Skilfully mass-produced for gluing to boxes and so on. Characteristic of Tunbridge Wells region where small wood turnery souvenirs for spa visitors existed from 17th century. Regency geometrical patterns such as 'three-dimensional' diamonds and long triangles (**477**); followed by mosaics, creating views (**478**: view of Knole), flower patterns and so on wholly in tiny squares, comparable with Berlin wool embroidery (smaller details illustrate flower in mosaic and napkin ring of 'stick work').

Turkey work 17th-early 18th centuries. Tufted upholstery usually with formalised flower patterns used for chair seats, cushions and so on, tougher than luxury velvets. Professional work, with pile hand-knotted on to canvas ground or woven by a carpet-making technique.

Turnery From earliest days. Chairs, stools, tables, small wares, more simply constructed than joiners' work. Wood shaped by being revolved against cutting tools, using pole-lathe or bow-lathe powered by foot-treadle or throw-lathe powered by assistant turning wheel.

Twiffler Potter's name for pudding plate.

Tyg Formerly Staffordshire term for porringer. Now collectors' term for drinking cup with two or more handles (**479**). Corresponding number of drinkers could share it, using different parts of rim. Sometimes two handles not diametrically opposite but convenient for couple seated side by side.

Underglaze colours Metallic oxides for ceramic ornament protected by covering of clear glaze. Heat of glazing kiln limited palette. See also *High temperature colours*.

Uranium For colouring glass, ceramics. From 1840s oxide of this rare metallic element used for golden-green colour such as 'vaseline glass'. Later for brilliant vermilion and orange ceramic glazes until prohibited as health hazard; hence no reproductions.

Usk japanning From 1761 when two brothers of Allgood family started japanning tin-plated iron at Usk, Monmouth, rivalling long-famous works at *Pontypool* (q.v.) and declaring themselves original makers of Pontypool japan which could survive unscathed in heat of charcoal fire. Urns, kettle braziers, chestnut servers, trays and so on. Closed 1860. (**480**: candlestick, its base decorated in 'Stormont' meander pattern).

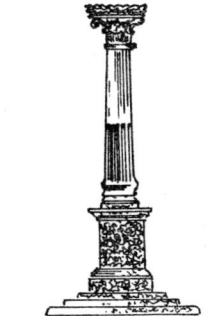

480 Usk japan candlestick

Valentine On sale from 1761. Ancient custom widely popular 19th century. Flimsy folded paper with verse, picture, printed and hand-coloured, followed by Victorian development of high-quality embossing, tinsel, paper lace **(481)**, elaborations of shells, wax flowers, feathers. Surprise pictures, transformation scenes, perfumed artificial flowers and relief effects with motifs mounted on tiny paper springs, requiring special boxes. In contrast, many cheap, often vulgar-comic, especially with anonymity available with penny post in 1840. Bank notes and postal order designs prohibited from 1872.

481 Embossed and painted valentine folding to envelope shape

Vallance (1) Wood, on furniture, used to conceal constructional detail: alternative term for apron or skirting. (2) Fabric hung from cornice to conceal curtain tops as on curtained bed, when it was linked by cantons at the corners. Lower vallances around bed frame below mattress known also as bases.

Varnish Transparent liquid which dries and hardens to protect furniture surface. Earliest had base of oil (linseed, poppy or walnut), long continued on cheap japanned furniture, also pictures. From late 17th-century spirit varnish (spirits of wine and gum lac) applied repeatedly and rubbed down and polished; improved later 18th century. Largely outmoded by French polish which became popular *c.* 1820.

Vauxhall glass From 1615. Glasshouse at Vauxhall, Lambeth, under Robert Mansell (monopoly from 1623), made drinking glasses, looking-glass. Revived 1665 (owned by Duke of Buckingham) producing mirror glass, very thin at first, less than $\frac{1}{4}$ in. thick and with wide shallow bevels. Closed 1780.

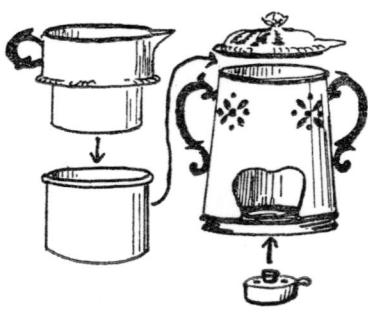

482 *Veilleuse*, showing typical five-part composition

Veilleuse Bedside food warmer for posset or caudle. From early Georgian through Victorian days, delft ware, cream wares, 19th-century bone china, stoneware, occasionally metal-lined wood. Cylindrical pedestal with side aperture for small lamp and open top to support lidded vessel above it which in 19th century was often protected from cracking by an under-vessel containing water (482 shows the five parts). Lid may support taper socket, or vessel may be handled and spouted as soup jug or pot for herb tea. Reproductions include Continental work in hard-paste porcelain.

Veneer From 17th century. Furniture enrichment achieved by covering wooden carcase with thin sheets of wood cut to show fine patterns of grain including irregular growths of burr and root (214). These saw cut (now knife cut) and skilfully glued to carcase surface, concealing constructional detail. Chosen for beauty of colour and grain regardless of strength.

'Venetian' glass Victorian, stimulated by exhibitions such as 1850 Society of Arts and 1867 Paris. Included contrastingly gilded and frosted; *millefiori* work such as paperweights (279); filigree mesh effects, white or coloured, within clear glass, known as latticinio; coloured glass threads binding surface of glass stems (418), handles.

Verre églomisé Mainly around 1700; especially as looking glass borders. Ornament on glass created by painting in gold on underside and backing with more glass and coloured foil.

Verzelini, G. 1522–1606, working in London 1570s–92. Important Venetian who established manufacture of Anglo-Venetian glass – thin blown, low temperature *lime-soda glass* such as blown glass table ware.

Vesica Late 18th-century's popular 'shuttle shape' – pointed oval formed of two intersecting circles, associated with Gothic architecture but better known to collectors as engraved and cut ornament on Irish glass, especially from Cork glasshouses (483: water jug).

Vickers metal From 1770s. When new, silvery white with faint tinge of blue, evolved by John Vickers, Sheffield (484), as a hard leadless form of pewter (mainly tin with a little antimony and copper). Mark: I VICKERS, small until 1817. After 1837 address added BRITANNIA PLACE SHEFFIELD. Somewhat more like silver, with finer texture, than *Britannia metal* (q.v.).

Victorian art pottery Important to today's

483 Vesica pattern on Irish water jug

484 Vickers metal version of 'Castleford' teapot

485 Victorian art pottery (Ault, of Swadlincote)

collector. Imaginative artist-designer work led by *Doulton, Minton, Wedgwood* and others. Also minor firms, especially from 1860 onwards, influenced by such professional designers as Christopher Dresser (e.g. Linthorpe, Middlesbrough **(486)**, 1870s–82 under Henry Tooth and *Bretby*, q.v.). Others to note include *Aller Vale* (q.v.); Barum, Barnstable from 1879 **(400)**; Sir Edmund Elton 1880s–1920; *Della Robbia* (q.v.); *W. De Morgan* (q.v.); Swadlincote, Derbyshire (W. Ault) from 1887 **(485)**. Less sophisticated wares such as slip with traditional yellowish glaze (sometimes greenish in 19th century) at *Fishley* (q.v.); various potteries around Rye, Sussex **(487, 488)**; Denholm, Yorks; *Castle Hedingham* (q.v.).

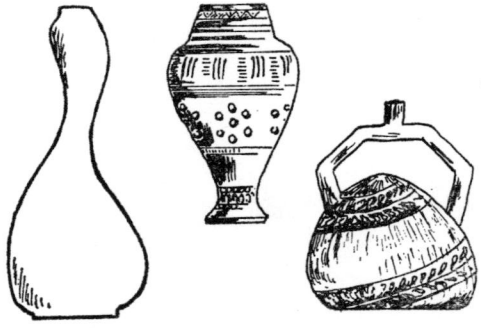

486 Victorian art pottery (three ornaments by Tooth, of Linthorpe)

Vignette Small decorative design, portrait or view which, instead of a border, has the edges shading off. Found in book chapter headings, Victorian writing paper (**489**: from wood engraving by T. Bewick, 1753–1828).

Vile, William d. 1767. In partnership with John Cobb: important cabinet makers and upholsterers making superbly-finished furniture splendidly enriched with carving in the rococo manner.

487–488 Victorian traditional country wares – Sussex pig with removable head and Rye vase

164

Vinaigrette From late 18th century. Mainly silver-gilt, silver. Tiny box with perforated gilded inner lid for holding wisp of sponge soaked in refreshing aromatic vinegar. Many imitative forms such as flexible fish, also embossed views and other elaborate ornament on conventional box shapes (**490**).

Vitrine Late Victorian term for glass display case in use from second half 18th century for collectors' items. Many Victorian, ormolu-mounted, in 'Louis XV' manner.

489   Vignette, Bewick style

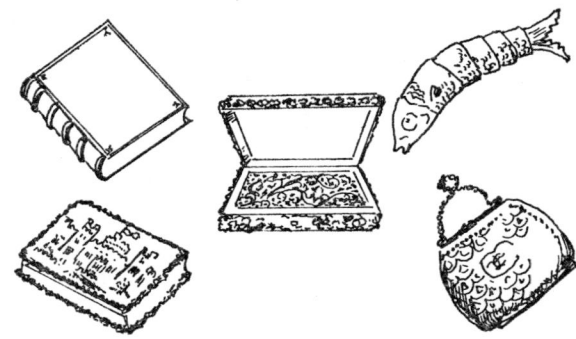

490   Vinaigrettes, silver

Voider 16th–17th century vessel for food scraps cleared from table after meal. Hence term for tray and by late 18th century especially for *butler's tray* (q.v.) resting on folding voider-stand.

Voyez, John, at work 1760s–90s. Important ceramic modeller who worked for Wedgwood, Ralph Wood, H. Palmer. Figures attributed to him often show unsmiling faces with wrinkled eyes and coarse lips (**465**).

491–492 Wall period Worcester porcelain: so-called Blind Earl pattern and cabbage leaf jug

493 Walton type earthenware – figure of Britannia

Wainscot From at least as early as 14th century, common term implying oak logs split and adze-cut to give boards of 8–10 in. face, largely imported 16th–17th centuries from Baltic ports; used for furniture and panelling. Important trade in wainscot billets through 18th–19th centuries but by then word applied to substantial furniture or panelling of any wood.

Wall, Dr. One of fourteen partners in Worcester porcelain factory then known as Worcester Tonquin Manufactory, from its founding 1751 to his death 1776. Continued by works manager William Davis to 1783 so that wares of 1751–83 usually known as 'Dr. Wall period' Worcester. Marks included crescent and cursive W. See also *Worcester*. (**491**: so-called 'Blind Earl' or Earl of Coventry pattern; **492**: cabbage leaf jug, rounder of mask and body than thin Caughley version.)

Walnut From 16th century; popular with Victorians. Richly grained golden brown wood, English and Continental, most decorative when used in veneers cut from burr growths. Solid for chairs, cupboards, bedsteads; veneers on cabinet furniture. Continued in 18th-century use long after mahogany became popular.

Walnut, Virginia or black American and English grown, mostly used as solid wood, darker, straighter grain, sometimes made to resemble mahogany. Important from 1720 when French banned export of their walnut.

Walton, John 1806–35. Burslem potter specialising in brittle earthenware figures often with crudely modelled bocage background, typically a few branches of huge oakleaves with V-shaped tips (**493**). Often tall mound plinth with relief scrolls giving name of subject on front and WALTON impressed on back. Many reproductions.

Warming pan From 16th century; some remain from early 17th century. Long-handled pan of coarse English brass to hold hot charcoal, with *latten* (q.v.) lid, slightly convex, embossed, engraved, pierced: to be thrust down bed for brief airing **(494 behind)**. More from *c.* 1720, lighter weight. In copper, early 18th century, with lid in beefeater-hat shape; from *c.* 1770, shallower, lighter, with curved lid (shaped by stamping) fitting inside rim of ember pan **(front)**. Rare in silver.

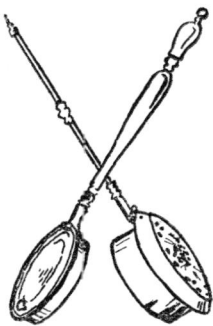

494   Warming pans, their lids of latten (*behind*) and copper

Warwick vase Classic marble vase over five feet high excavated Tivoli and brought to Warwick Castle by Earl, 1774. Bronze replicas made by Sir Edward Thomason *c.* 1820. Copies in silver by Paul Storr, 1812; in Sheffield plate by I. & I. Waterhouse and others as wine coolers **(495)**, soup tureens and so on from 1820s: several exhibited 1851.

495   Warwick vase design adapted as wine cooler

Wash-basin stand **(496)** 18th to early 19th century tripod stand with ring of wood for basin and lower shelf recess for soap or wig powder box. Soon more flowing lines, squarer. Many with elaborate fitments concealed under folding lids and cupboard fronts for dual-purpose rooms: these continued into Victorian days. See also *Wig stand*.

Wassail bowl From 17th century, bowl for serving Christmas and Twelfth Night drinks, large because newly popular *lignum vitae* wood (q.v.) was dense enough to turn into deep bowls more than 12 inches across. Occasionally silver mounted and lidded; sometimes accompanied by turned wood tumblers. Present-day specimens turned in traditional styles.

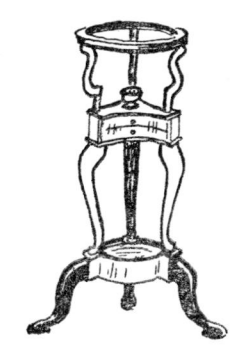

496   Wash-basin stand

497 Watch stand in papier mâché

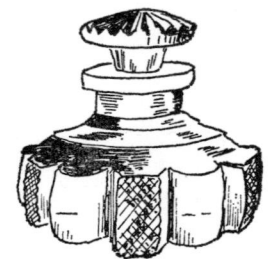

498 Waterford glass

499 Watermark, 18th century

500 Waxjack, silver

Watch stand Late 18th century onwards. Wood, ceramics. Frame with aperture to hold watch, serving as mantel or bedside clock. Included such designs as turreted castles, grandfather clocks and Victorian flat-back figure groups (**497**: papier mâché thermometer).

Waterford glass (G. & W. Penrose.) Important from 1784 when Stourbridge glassmakers under John Hill went there, taking advantage of Irish freedom from tax-by-weight then hampering English flint-glass. Law altered 1825. Heavy, lavish work (**498**: toilet water bottle) but glass itself difficult to distinguish from English and responding to similar fashions. Waterford also imported and sold English glass. Other glass centres at Dublin, Belfast, Cork. Occasional marks.

Watermarks Line patterns, letters, numbers, visible in substance of paper held against light (**499**). Introduced in course of paper manufacture. May include date which can help to establish age of old pattern book, print, map, but must be viewed with caution as can be faked.

Waxjack 18th century, silver (**500**), brass. Open frame with central spool vertical or horizontal to hold coil of flexible wax taper. End of taper secured vertically in clip to provide glimmer of flame for sealing, smoking. Soon extinguished itself if unattended. Towards end of century thinner taper and plainer holder. See also *Bougie box*.

Wax models From 18th century for ceramic use, might serve as basis for master mould which provided numerous moulds for shaping the parts of figure, assembled before kiln firing. Wedgwood used those of Flaxman, Hackwood and others for medallions and so on in jasper ware, basaltes. See also *Cire perdue*.

Wax portraits Ancient craft most popular in 18th century. Beeswax discoloured with age: a usual alternative consisted of white wax mixed with turpentine and flake white tinted with vermilion. Wax effigies of dead followed by portraits from which copies could be cast in plaster; also preparatory studies for sculpture. Portrait mounted on oval of glass, wax, velvet or silk. Important artists included Samuel Percy (1750–1820), I. Gosset, P. Rouw, T. R. Poole, R. C. Lucas. See also *Tassie medallions*.

Wedgwood, Josiah 1730–95. World-famous English potter, his manufactory still in production, including wares and patterns created under his leadership. Made no porcelain but endless experiments led to invention and improvement of many bodies and glazes, notably cream-coloured earthenware, early 1760s (see also *Queen's ware*), black basaltes (**26**), 1765, jasper ware (**231**), 1774, pearl ware, 1779. Etruria factory near Stoke-on-Trent established 1769. (**501**: Cauliflower ware. Other illustrations: **204, 269, 322, 335, 345.**)

Wedgwood marks Nearly always *WEDG-WOOD* or *Wedgwood*; occasionally *W & B* while in partnership with Thomas Bentley, 1769–80. From 1860 firm might use group of three impressed letters representing date of manufacture. Name *Wedgewood* (with middle e) and occasionally *J. Wedgwood* noted on wares made by firm of W. Smith & Co., Stockton-on-Tees, 1826–50s. Mark *Wedgwood & Co.* used by Tunstall firm from 1860s when Josiah's successors were Josiah Wedgwood & Sons Ltd.

Wednesbury enamels From 1770s until *c.* 1840, pioneered by Samuel Yardley. Long neglected source of many painted enamel toys, still frequently ascribed to *Battersea* and *Bilston* (qq.v.) including press-shaped, embossed articles enamelled by dipping before ornamenting with transfer-print and/or hand colouring (**502**: etui).

Weights and measures marks From 1824 when imperial system of weights and measures introduced and tavern keepers, shell fish sellers and so on had to use measuring vessels officially tested and marked. In pottery such as *mocha ware* (q.v.) potter indicated vessel's capacity (**503**) and weights and measures officer added verification stamp such as zinc band on handle or metal plug under lip.

Weights and measures, standard mark In 1878 Board of Trade ordered standard mark: royal crown over monarch's cypher and a number indicating county or borough – such as 522 for London, 19 for Derbyshire, 10 for Cornwall. Later, capacity included in stencilled mark, applied to ceramic or glass by acid or sand blasting (**504**).

Wellington chest Popular 19th century. Tall narrow chest of as many as 12 shallow drawers all secured by a hinged vertical wooden flap which could be locked.

Welsh dresser Name from Victorian days for dresser in 18th-century style of handsomely framed open shelves above a long draw-

501 Wedgwood cauliflower ware, 1759 design

502 Wednesbury enamel etui

503–504 Weights and measures: two marks embossed by potters (*top*) and standard design from 1878

505 Welsh dresser

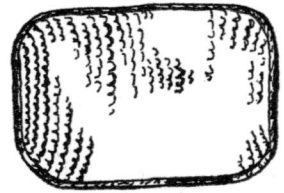

506 Welsh ware meat dish

507 Williamite glass

508 Willow pattern

er-fitted table top but with cupboards filling the space between drawers and floor (505).

Welsh love-spoon   See *Love-spoon*.

Welsh ware   Some 18th century, more 19th century. Large oblong meat dishes in coarse earthenware characteristically covered with combed or feathered zigzag patterns in contrasting light and dark tones of clay slip (506).

Welted foot   Glass. From late 17th century, usual to 1750 and found also in some 19th-century glasses and many reproductions. Foot rim of drinking glass strengthened by being folded in on itself – upwards at first (folded foot) but more often downwards.

Whatnot   See *Omnium*.

Wheel or dial barometer   From 1720s: fashionable from 1760s through most of 19th century, including popular *banjo* form (q.v.). Register plate was circular 'clock face', frequently silvered and covered with convex glass, the mercury tube cased in mahogany or rosewood. Regency case often included additional features such as hygrometer, thermometer, clock and – to ensure erect hanging – spirit level.

Wheel engraving   See *Engraved glass*.

Whieldon, Thomas   *c.* 1719–95. Important Staffordshire potter with factory at Fenton Low from 1740. Partnership with Wedgwood 1754–9. No marked work but some collectors attribute to him much of period's best tortoiseshell (471), agate and marbled wares.

Wig stand   Very rare. Rounded wooden knob or 'mushroom' on stemmed stand. Occasionally ceramic dome. Name more often given, incorrectly, to small wash basin stand (q.v.) provided in wig-powdering closet.

Williamite glass   Decanters, drinking vessels associated with William of Orange (English king 1689–1702) and inscribed THE GLORIOUS MEMORY (507). But mostly engraved after 1780 – some on old glass – following founding of Orange Institution. Engraving of equestrian portrait from Van Nost statue associated with appointment of Duke of York as Institution's grand master, 1822.

Willow pattern   From *c.* 1780. Pseudo-Chinese design introduced by Thomas Turner, Caughley, as blue transfer-printed ornament on table wares, at first with no figures on bridge. Similar patterns by Spode from 1785, Wedgwood from 1795; other users including Davenport, William Adams and Swansea. Thomas Minton, when freelance etcher of copper plates, supplied variants to other potters (**508**: typical of later designs by Spode, Minton and others).

Wilton carpets From early 18th century manufactured at Wilton, Wiltshire; close-pile, 'velvet' weave of Brussels from 1740s; Axminster looms acquired 1835. See also *Axminster carpet*.

Windsor chair Through 18th–19th centuries and much reproduced. Primitive construction based on lathe turning of local woods, especially Buckinghamshire. Back uprights and splayed 'stick' legs (ash or beech) taper-tenoned into block of non-splitting elm wood shaped as *saddle seat* (q.v.). Comb-back variety with wavy-topped crest rail supported by row of plain spindles (**509**). Soon followed by hoop-back with spindles enclosed by vertical bow of wood tenoned into horizontal bow cross-rail which was extended to form arm rests (**510**). In low-back variant without arms the hooped rail was socketed into seat. Sturdy for stone floors, especially when made of resilient yew and ash. Some cabriole legs around 1750–70; some rounded cow's horn or spur stretchers, late 18th century (**510**). Several regional variants. Simple versions made as kitchen chairs or 'white wycombes' through 19th century.

509–510 Windsor chairs: comb-back (*top*) and hoop back

Wine bottles Some bear seals and dates (**384**). Early and to end of 18th century in thinly-blown green glass, rounded at base, originally protected with osier. Alternative, 17th to early 18th century: thick, dark glass: blown and tooled in long-necked shaft-and-globe shape to 1750s and mould-shaped (dappled surface) in short-necked cylindrical version. Taller in 1760s, with 5 in. diameter, becoming still taller with 3 in. diameter towards 1800. String-rim at mouth replaced 1820s–40s by broad sloping lip, with introduction of machine-moulding.

Wine coaster From 1750s to protect table from rub of bottle or decanter. Flat base (boxwood from *c.* 1775) and low vertical rim (silver, Sheffield plate, wood) to fit bottle base or more expensive decanter. Some double coasters from 1790s; florid from 1820s, including footed variants from 1830s. (**511**: jolly boat, Sheffield plate, *c.* 1825.)

511 Double wine coaster

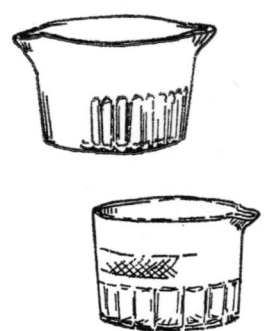

512 Two wine glass coolers

513 Wine labels: designs introduced about 1770s and 1820s

514 Wine label variants: Battersea enamel (1750s) and letter by Dixon (1860s)

515 Wine waiter

Wine glass cooler About 1750–1860, for individual wine glasses as distinct from *monteith* (q.v.). Distinguished from finger bowl (used from 1760s) by one or two lips in rim for wine glass stem (**512**). Blue glass from 1780s, ruby and green from 1820s.

Wine label From 1720s, silver, Sheffield plate, for hanging by chain around bottle neck; later also for decanter. At first, plain rectangles and ovals inscribed with names of liquors (sometimes sauces, essences). Pierced, crested from 1770s (**513 left**), embossed from 1790s. From 1770s into 19th century elaborate versions for decanters, hand raising soon supplemented by die-stamping and 19th-century's heavy castings. Perforated letters in vine leaves from 1824 (**513 right**).

Wine label variants From 1780s, plain neck rings engraved with wine names. Single letter labels from *c.* 1820 becoming ornate (**514**) and including rows of letters by 1835. Other labels in 18th-century painted enamels, much copied (**514 top**); 18th–19th century, ivory, including ivory chain and ivory neck ring, mother of pearl, china, bone, engraved tiger's tooth or boar's tusk or pair of tiger claws, silver harnessed. Bottle stopper with labelled silver cap, 1825–60. All outmoded by fashion for claret jugs and for bottles with printed labels resulting from 1860 Grocers' Licences Act.

Wine waiter From later 18th century. Cellaret, for storing bottles when sideboard lacked cupboards. Somewhat resembling canterbury music stand but partitioned into squares (**515**: sarcophagus shape).

Wire work Silver, Sheffield plate. Mainly *c.* 1785–1815. In Sheffield plate silver was fused under heat upon copper then drawn into wire of required thickness and shaped into cake baskets, epergnes, toast racks and so on. The wire, drawn to attractive cross-sections, was used at first in short lengths, soldered into position (**516**); from *c.* 1800 in long pieces curved into patterns.

Witch ball From later 18th century. Cheap glass ornament in Nailsea styles ranging from dark bottle glass flecked or spotted to light glass containing transfer-printed pictures backed by opaque white and marbled colours. Some silvered inside. Many lack openings. Sometimes confused with dark glass ball floats used for fishermen's nets.

Woodcut Simple form of *relief print* (q.v.).

Mainly plain outlines, little depth or shadow. Well suited to broadsides and the like, printed on poor paper.

Wood engraving Mainly from later 18th century onwards, popularised by Thomas Bewick (1735–1828). Refinement of woodcut with greater detail and tone range.

Wood family Staffordshire potters. Ralph (1715–72) followed by son (1748–95) and grandson (all same name) to 1801. His brother Aaron (1717–85) followed by son Enoch (1759–1840) and Enoch's sons (active 1780s–1846). The Ralph Woods were associated with figures including successive types of toby jugs; Aaron with fine cutting of moulds for potters; Enoch with large figures and also transfer-printed useful wares, including marked work by the partnership Wood & Caldwell. (**517**: export ware, E. Wood & Sons, *c.* 1835 showing ship with U.S. flag seen from mouth of cave which forms plate rim.)

Worcester porcelain factory Established 1751 (see *Dr. Wall* above) becoming Royal Worcester Porcelain Co. in 1788. Noted for particularly fine soapstone porcelain table wares (**64**) and vases, ornately coloured, meticulously gilded (**518**: 'dishevelled bird' on tea jar); also bone china from *c.* 1800, later parian, ivory porcelain and so on. Some confusion with Caughley. From 1783 under Thomas Flight; Flight & Barr, 1792–1807; Barr, Flight & Barr, 1807–13; Flight, Barr & Barr (**519**) 1813–40. Amalgamated with Robert Chamberlain (see also *Chamberlain, Worcester*) in 1840 (**520**), the firm styled Chamberlain & Co., 1840–52; *Kerr & Binns* 1852–62 (q.v.). Thereafter Worcester Royal Porcelain Co. Ltd., taking over factory of *Thomas Grainger* (q.v.) in 1889. Initials in marks aid dating (Two of many marks, **270**).

516 Wire-work basket

517 Wood family: transfer-printed plate by E. Wood & Sons, *c.* 1835

518 Worcester porcelain, Wall period (dishevelled bird)

519 Worcester, Flight, Barr & Barr (shell ornament)

520 Worcester, Chamberlain (feather ornament)

Wreathing Some porcelain, stoneware and earthenware. Spiralling ridges inside thrown vessel, finger-formed in course of shaping and often regarded as defect but might be introduced deliberately as slight interior corrugation strengthened vessel through firing process. Conspicuous in early stoneware such as hard-to-clean bellarmines.

Wrought iron Distinguished by collector from more brittle cast iron. Tough, malleable, resistant to corrosion (**101; 521**: I & J. Taylor *c.* 1795). Shaped by heating and hammering – the blacksmith's craft – or by traditional locksmith methods of cutting and filing.

521 Wrought iron lamp (I. & J. Taylor, *c.* 1795)

Yard-arm barometer 1670 design by Sir Samuel Morland, especially popular 1720–40s. Often in squarish wooden frame (sometimes central looking-glass) allowing mercury tube to rise vertically at one side and continue across the top at slight slant so that small variations in atmospheric pressure caused considerable movement along it, permitting great accuracy in reading.

Yard-of-ale glass 18th-century version was flute ending in ball knop and highly domed welted foot: in 19th century knop omitted and foot flat. Trick form, popular 1830s–40s, with hollow bulb at base of flute (**522**).

Yellow glaze ware Like *green glaze ware* (q.v.) developed by young Wedgwood 1750s. Often noted with surface relief patterns and combined with green in vegetable and pineapple forms.

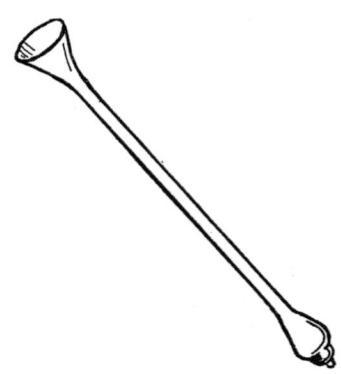

522 Yard of ale trick glass

Yew wood Reddish brown, hard, elastic for resilient country furniture (e.g. Windsor chairs). Burr veneer has curly grain suggesting amboyna.

Yorkshire-Derbyshire chairs Introduced 17th century but popular in reproductions. Plain oak chair in square shape of period but with open back dominated by arched or arcaded top rail, sometimes with turned spindles or arched cross rail (523).

Yorkshire dresser Popular name for 19th-century style with clock high in shelving.

523 'Yorkshire-Derbyshire' chair

Zaffre Cobalt oxide, discovered Saxony 1545, used for blue painting and printing ceramics. See also *Smalt*. Over-purification in 19th century detracted from quality of colour.